Chiara Ingrosso

essays by

Laura Andreini
Josep Maria Montaner
Ton Salvadó
Alessandro Scarnato

ON THE ROAD city
Barcelona

ON THE ROAD
Editor of collection
Laura Andreini

editorial project
Forma Edizioni srl, Firenze, Italia
redazione@formaedizioni.it
www.formaedizioni.it

editorial direction
Laura Andreini

author
Chiara Ingrosso

editorial staff
Maria Giulia Caliri
Livia D'Aliasi
Andrea Benelli

graphic design
Isabella Peruzzi
Alessandra Smiderle

translations
Katy Hannan
Graham Robertson for NTL,
Florence

photolithography
LAB di Gallotti Giuseppe Fulvio,
Florence

First Edition: February 2019

ISBN 978-88-99534-72-1

texts by
Laura Andreini
Josep Maria Montaner
Ton Salvadó
Alessandro Scarnato

Roberto Cosenza: pp. 30, 34-38, 44, 50, 64, 74, 90-94, 136, 166, 176, 180, 204
Chiara Ingrosso: pp. 28, 32, 36, 40, 46-48, 52-54, 60-62, 66-68, 70-72, 76-88, 96-108, 164
Aurora Maria Riviezzo: pp. 112-134, 138-154, 158-162, 168-178, 182-202, 206-208

Chiara Ingrosso is an Architect and assistant Professor in History of Architecture at the Department of Architecture and Design of the University of Campania Luigi Vanvitelli, where she teaches History of Architecture and Design. She won scholarships and she taught at various international universities, among which: Barcelona, Istanbul, Beijing and Johannesburg. She is author of essays and monographs published in Italy and abroad

With the support of:

Ajuntament de Barcelona

Table of contents

Guidebook as tool

On the Road is a collection of contemporary architecture guidebooks whose purpose is to tell about a place, whether a city or larger area, through its architectural works chosen to be visited and experienced directly.

The guidebook has a convenient special jacket that opens into a map marking the location of the architectural works and interesting sites to visit. On the back are miniature images and addresses of the architectural works described in detail within.

The book starts with short essays explaining the city or area's present day and history and outlining possible future scenarios with planned or imminent projects. Each work features a photograph of the whole, an architectural drawing (plan or section), a short description, and facts including architect, type, year of construction, address, website, and how to visit it.

The finest architecture of each city and suggested routes are represented by this collection of not-to-be-missed, "timeless" buildings that uniquely define their settings. General information and useful tips for travelers help them optimize their visits and quickly understand the essence of the place described.

Museums, theatres, restaurants, hotels and a list of top architectural firms working in the city let visitors turn a regular trip into an opportunity for study or work.

Note: The pinpoints outside the maps at the beginning of the itineraries are viewable on the rear of the book jacket.

Barcelona

Laura Andreini*

* Architect and Associate Professor at DIDA, University of Florence. Co-founder of Studio Archea where she still works, she is also writer and Deputy Editor for *area* magazine

The first Spanish city to be explored in the On the Road series is Barcelona, a metropolis that has demonstrated for decades a strong international quality, because of its geographical position, its important port, and because of its competitive desire to distinguish itself in a certain way from the capital, Madrid.

One of the most interesting aspects of contemporary Barcelona lies in the integration of its outstanding architectural interventions within a clearly defined urban plan. This began back in the late 1980s when Barcelona was preparing to host the 1992 Olympic Games, and in the new urban layouts of certain areas, constellations of archistar interventions changed the configuration of the Barcelona skyline. For years, the city has played a leading role in the most important publications of architecture and urban planning; vast redevelopment projects have modernised important areas of the city, and after a short pause caused by the economic crisis in 2008, today, Barcelona has made a comeback with its avant-garde social and urban planning policies.

In the last ten years, but especially since 2015, the Barcelona municipal administration has focused careful attention on improving public spaces. In fact, Barcelona is a city famous for its intense urban lifestyle, and public policy has decided to defend and encourage this characteristic quality. In recent years, the focus has moved from archistar landmarks to projects of excellence, integrating external spaces, an aspect that should never be underestimated.

Barcelona is following a route to transform itself into a green city promoting sustainable transport, over private vehicles. The increase in green urban spaces also facilitates better integration of local populations within their neighbourhood or area, aimed at accomodating the increasing tourist population, without sacrificing the living space and quality of life of the locals. The best way to visit a city is to share the lifestyle of its people, and Barcelona is a city that provides this experience to the fullest.

The tour visits eighty-six projects, each in this book in detail, and is divided into four itineraries. The divisions are aimed at encouraging visitors to explore individual "quarters", to view the best examples of contemporary architecture, and at the same time, to take the time to stroll, ride a bike, or travel on public transport to enjoy the experience of such a high quality urban centre.

Political / geographical facts

country
Spain

language
Catalan
Spanish

area code
+34 93

coordinates
41° 23 N
2° 10 E

area
101.4 sq. km

population
1,620,809

density
15,984 inhabitants / sq.km

time zone
UTC+1

city website
www.barcelona.cat

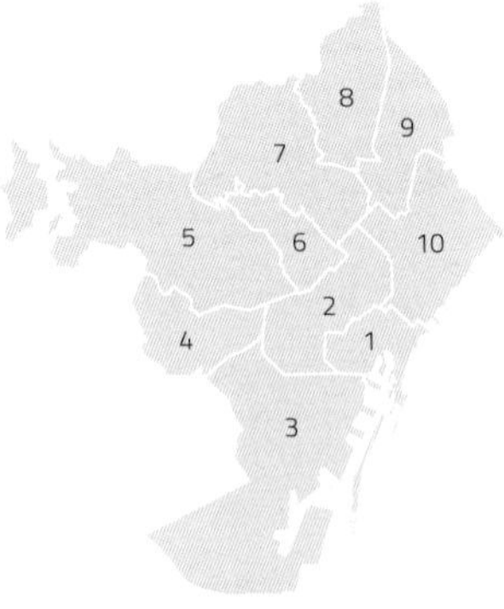

Administrative districts

1. Ciutat Vella
2. Eixample
3. Sants-Montjuïc
4. Les Corts
5. Sarrià-Sant Gervasi
6. Gràcia
7. Horta-Guinardó
8. Nou Barris
9. Sant Andreu
10. Sant Martí

General information
useful addresses and numbers

INFORMATION OFFICES*

www.barcelonaturisme.com

Plaça Catalunya
Plaça de Catalunya, 17
+34 93 285 38 34
daily / 8.30 am - 9 pm

Plaça Sant Jaume
Plaça de Sant Jaume, Ciutat, 2
+34 93 285 38 34
Mon - Fri / 8.30 am - 8 pm
Sat / 9 am - 8 pm
Sun, holidays / 9 am - 3 pm

Estació de Sants
Plaça dels Països Catalans
daily / 8.30 am - 8.30 pm

Terminal Aeroporto 1 e 2
Aeroporto El Prat (terminal 1 e 2B)
daily / 8.30 am - 8.30 pm

Oficina Catedral
Plaça Nova, 5 (Col·legi Oficial d'Arquitectes de Catalunya. COAC)
Mon - Sat / 9 am - 7 pm
Sun, holidays / 9 am - 3 pm

EMERGENCY SERVICES

Police, Fire Department, Emergency medical service 112
Spanish National Police 091
Emergency medical service 061
Fire Department 080

URBAN TRANSPORT**

Bus and Tram
tickets: can be purchased at ticket windows, automatic ticket vending machines, information desks, and TMB info points
www.tmb.cat

Subway (12 city lines)
tickets: can be purchased at ticket windows, automatic ticket vending machines, information desks, and TMB info points
www.tmb.cat

Taxi
Associació Ràdio Taxi Miramar: +34 93 433 10 20
Cooperativa de Ràdio Taxi Metropolitana de Barcelona: +34 93 225 00 00
Ràdio Taxi 033: +34 93 303 30 33
Servi Taxi: +34 93 330 03 00
Taxi Groc: +34 93 322 22 22

Car sharing
Ubeeqo, Bluemove, Avancar, Socialcar, Drivy

GENERAL CONSULATE OF UNITED STATES OF AMERICA
Paseo Reina Elisenda de Montcada, 23 - 08034 Barcelona
Contact centre +34 93 280 22 27

GENERAL CONSULATE OF CHINA
Carrer de Lleó XIII, 34 - 08022, Barcelona
Contact centre +34 93 254 70 70

GENERAL CONSULATE OF ITALY
Calle de Mallorca, 270 - 08037, Barcelona
Contact centre +34 90 205 01 41

BRITISH CONSULATE
Avinguda Diagonal, 477- 08036, Barcelona
Contact centre +34 93 366 62 00

GENERAL CONSULATE OF FRANCE
Ronda Universitat, 22 - 08007, Barcelona
Contact centre +34 93 270 30 49

GENERAL CONSULATE OF RUSSIA
Avinguda Pearson, 34 - 08034, Barcelona
Contact centre +34 93 280 02 20

HOW TO PHONE

from a local landline: dial the area code (93) and then the number

from a foreign landline: dial the international code (+34), city code (93) and number

* As well as information offices, there are several tourist information kiosks located in strategic areas around the city that offer personal service.

** Ticket categories:
standard ticket, 10-trip ticket (T10, this can be used for Metro, bus and tram travel) the Hola BCN! pass, Barcelona Card, daily travel pass.

Useful tips

1. Barcelona is a city with a vast hospitality industry. In the city centre, especially in areas like Ciutat Vella but also in the Eixample district, there are a large number of hotels for every taste and category, including gay hotels. The exponential increase in **B&Bs**, specifically set up and managed by *ad hoc* companies, has been countered by certain policies promoted by the City Council in recent years, mainly because it has led to widespread gentrification. In other words, the local population has been displaced to create tourist accommodation, resulting in the conversion of entire streets or urban areas exclusively for this purpose. For this reason, it is advisable to take care when selecting structures that are sensitive to these issues and which comply with the criteria of the responsible and sustainable cultural tourism established by the City Council, all of which can be accessed on the appropriate Web page.

2. For travel around Barcelona, there is a very efficient public bus and rail transport system. The subway (**metropolitana**), recently completed with new lines and stations, is the most common form of transport used by the local population; almost all the itineraries proposed in the guide can be reached by subway, but a bus ride is also a useful way to view the city. Breathtaking views can be had from the cable way (**Teleferica**) that connects the Paral·lel with the Montjuïc hill.

3. The city offers a vast cultural choice with a large range of museums, like the famous **Museu Picasso,** the **Fundació Joan Miró/43**, the **Museu d'Art Contemporani de Barcelona (MACBA)/07** and the **Centre de Cultura Contemporània de Barcelona (CCCB)/07**, and the more recent **Museu del Disseny/20**. We also recommend the interesting **Museu d'Història de Barcelona** and the **Museu de la Música de Barcelona** (located inside the **Auditori de Barcelona/18**).

4. The open markets of Barcelona are well worth a visit. Markets can be found in almost every neighbourhood. They are not only for buying fresh produce, but also include fascinating places for second-hand bargains. Many markets also serve fresh and cooked foods, like the **Mercat di Santa Caterina/08** in Ribera or many of the stalls at the more crowded Mercat de Sant Josep de la Boqueria, more commonly called **La Boqueria**, in the centre of les Rambles. The **Mercat Fira de Bellcaire Els Encants/19** near Plaça de les Glòries Catalanes is the city's most famous Flea Market, which has replaced the old flea market that previously existed in the neighbourhood.

5. Barcelona has a large number of parks, large and small, in every district. Very often they are the result of the transformation of abandoned areas, an initiative started in the 1980s. There were few public parks in the former compact Barcelona urban fabric; these included the **Ciutadella**, the **Parc de Montjuïc** and the **Park Güell/75** by Gaudí. The new parks, such as the **Parc de l'Espanya Industrial** and **Parc dell'Escorxador** are very popular with the public.

6. Public spaces in Barcelona are not limited to its parks. The city is rich in public squares. The city centre has endless small "hard squares" or paved areas, furnished simply with benches or a fountain. In Gràcia, it is worth spending some time in pleasant squares like **Plaça del Sol**, **Plaça Trilla**, **Plaça de la Virreina**, **Plaça Rius i Taulet**, while in the Barri Gòtic district, a visit to **Plaça Reial** should not be missed.

7. In the long warm summer season, people flock to the beaches along the Barcelona seafront. The beaches are often crowded, so it is better to avoid those near the central areas around Barceloneta. But even for those who do not want to swim, there are wonderful walks along the coast on the Passeig de Colom as far as the most eastern limits of Poblenou. This is an area well worth visiting to admire the impressive transformations that have been achieved along the whole Barcelona seafront.

8. The people of Barcelona love the theatre. The **Palau de la Música Catalana** is truly worth visiting, if only for its modernist architecture. The same applies to the celebrated **Gran Teatre del Liceu** on les Rambles, or the **Teatre Apolo** in the Poble-sec area. The famous old **Sala Beckett/31** was recently restored in the Poblenou quarter.

9. For fans of electronic and contemporary music, spring is a great season to visit Barcelona. The two international **Primavera Sound** and **Sonar** festivals are held every year between May and July. Festival concerts are performed in various areas around the city including the **Parc del Fòrum**, the **Fira Montjuïc** and the **Fira Gran Via de L'Hospitalet**.

Barcelona, a shared story

Josep Maria Montaner*

* Full Professor in Architectural Theory at the Escuela de Arquitectura de Barcelona (ETSAB-UPC), Councillor at the Barcelona Municipality Vivienda y Rehabilitación and Councillor for the district of Sant Martí

There is every good reason for claiming that Barcelona is evolving into a "post model"; her story is neither clear-cut nor hierarchical but is rich in open-minded and ambivalent points of view, a story that is not expressed through great works nor dreamt up or represented by a single person (Pascual Maragall, Oriol Bohigas...). Rather, it is increasingly created and shared by a whole political, social and technical movement, spread digitally, dynamically, in a spirit of collaboration. A story that is sparked off with discussion, in each district of the city, led for the first time by a woman, Ada Colau. What we have is a model based on redistribution and regeneration aimed at recreating the very weft of the urban fabric. A model that reclaims and consolidates the public sphere, stipulating that public spaces should absolutely remain as they are; at the same time it considers the home to be a public facility and views the city as being made up essentially of spaces for living. A compact city that must now stake everything on a process of regeneration. A redistributive "post model" that treats each place according to its specific qualities, thus potentiating the intensity of urban life, in line with the ideas put forward by Jane Jacobs. Priority has been given to the most neglected working-class areas of Besós and the North, as well as Raval and the future quarter of Marina del Prat Vermell. Further impulse has been added by a District Plan, which has resulted in dozens of urban and social renewal schemes, like the future head offices of the district of Sant Martí in El Besós, by the architect Jorge Vidal, who had already collaborated with Víctor Rahola on the construction of the Centro Cultural Teresa Pàmies, in Carrer Comte d'Urgell.

All this is bubbling up in a city that is gradually upgrading the standard and quality of her infrastructures: educational, like the schools designed by SUMO Arquitectes at Poblenou, or the Escuela Massana (School of Art and Design) in the Boquería, by Carme Pinós; libraries, such as the two designed by Josep Llinás (the Gracia Library and the one in Plaça Lesseps), or the library by the architects of the RCR Studio at Sant Antoni; and spaces devoted to culture, like Can Framis by Jordi Badia and the Sala Beckett, by Eva Prats and Ricardo Flores, both at Poblenou; or the Lleialtat Santsensa at La Bordeta, in the spaces redesigned by Harquitectes; or again, markets, from the Mercat de Santa Caterina, by Enric Miralles and Benedetta Tagliabue, to the one in Barceloneta by Josep Miàs, to the recently inaugurated Mercat de Sant Antoni, the work of Carme Ribas and Pere Joan Ravetllat.

With the aim of promoting an urban plan that functions more efficiently and ecologically, the need has been felt to speed up the processes that contribute to making a city that is green and that enhances styles of comunal living, within a framework of sustainable mobility: increasing the kilometres of cycle paths, revamping the bus network so that it runs orthogonally while still waiting for the completion of the tramway network; increasing walkways and green spaces, as planned along the Meridiana, and with the new "canopy" park of Las Glorias. Barcelona possesses a magnificent heritage of parks, some unusual, such as the Botanic Garden designed by the Carlos Ferrater Group, the Passeig de Sant Joan by Lola Domènech, and the fifty gardens enclosed within blocks of buildings. For the first time Barcelona is provided with a *Medida de igualdad de género en el proyecto urbano* (Measure for gender equality in urban planning) extended to housing policies, an essential tool for improving the quality of everyday life.

In parallel, there has been the need to give priority to tackling problems arising from mass tourism, by means of the PEUAT *Plan Especial Urbanístico de Alojamientos Turísticos* (Special Plan for tourist accommodation), with the aim of protecting traditional ways of life and the stability of the neighbourhood. The PEUAT is integrated with the *Plan por el derecho a la vivienda en Barcelona* (2016-2025) (Plan for the right to a home in Barcelona, 2016-2025), which envisages the doubling of public housing available in the next ten years.

Barcelona has been inspired by other models, from the "possibilist ecologism" of Curitiba to the pioneering sustainability of Seattle, and also intends to learn from, and exchange experiences with, capitals like New York, London, Paris, Berlin and Vienna. In the meantime the DNA of the city and her citizens is flourishing: creative, critical and innovative capacity, totally at the service of safeguarding the quality and development of her urban territory.

We are experimenting with a kind of town planning based on "common things", which values rights above cement and overbuilding; a narrative in which we are beginning to build an alternative model to Neoliberalism. An urban post model that is being put to the test as a strategic choice and harks back to the late nineteenth century neighbourhood project championed by pioneering women who defended community living and taught Patrick Geddes to rebuild and improve rather than demolish. Barcelona is at the forefront in this experience of change, a city conceived by thousands of minds that are experimenting daily on a small scale, district by district. And she intends to go on being a city of splendid architecture and to further enhance the quality of life in every single one of her urban spaces.

Barcelona, changing the rules of the game

Ton Salvadó*

* Director of the Department for the Urban Model of the City Council of Barcelona

As a result of the enormous transformation of the last forty years of democratric administration, Barcelona is now a well-structured entity, a pre-existing playing field: nevertheless, the great conflicts centring on an equitable distribution of urban space resources have necessitated a change in the game plan: so that the actual physical city must act as a support to people's lives. Faced with this challenge, we are working on a series of strategies that start from the city's equilibrium, based on cross-sectoral interventions, guiding us towards a new urban model whose primary objective is the well being of the inhabitants.

The issue, aimed at substantially increasing the number of green spaces, does not simply have the banal aim of beautifying the urban environment, but is, rather, one of the crucial mainstays for the life and survival of the citizens. We need more trees to improve the delicate CO2 equilibrium, to reduce the absorption surface and thermal inertia, to tackle the increase in temperature deriving from the heat-island effect and to protect public areas from the sun – and to ultimately enhance liveability and environmental quality. Approved plans for the Tres Turons park will make this area a core element in the process of urban greenery expansion in Barcelona.

With the aim of limiting private vehicle traffic in public spaces, thus contributing substantially to the reduction of pollution, noise and the risk of accidents, we are working on a scheme to restrict both the spaces available to traffic and the actual number of vehicles parked in the streets. All this entails an extensive and radical reconfiguration of the inner city areas, and in this context we find, *inter alia*, the project for transforming the Meridiana artery, which will prompt a reduction in areas permitting vehicle traffic, to the benefit of the pedestrian, as well as an increase in urban greenery and greater bicycle mobility.

On the other hand, we still have to guarantee general mobility, and for this reason we are busily engaged in improving the public transport system. One of the mainsprings will be the implementation of the orthogonal city bus network, in parallel with an extension of some as yet incomplete stretches of the metro line, as well as the execution of a project that will connect the two already-existing branches of the tramline across the Diagonal. This is the first step in the future expansion of this collective transport system, a far more sustainable option even if, for political reasons, it will be necessary to wait for a second mandate in the next City Council term.

Interest in developing sustainable mobility and fostering a shift in transport habits in the city (giving up the use of private vehicles) has also been shown in recent years in the creation of new bicycle-focused infrastructures, i.e., dedicated cycle lanes – which take up the spaces previously given over to traffic or parking – and boosting the public bike network – the so-called *Bicing*. However, the idea is especially to promote and facilitate transit on foot, and to rediscover the pleasure of walking, which, in our city with her compact urban fabric, would appear a logical and natural step.

And it is within this framework that the *superilles* come into play, large superblocks by means of which the city is transformed – a new kind of use of the city, taking back public spaces for the pedestrians. It is a question of maintaining an essential network of streets open to normal car traffic, while in all the interstitial streets within these great urban blocks vehicle traffic is limited solely to local traffic entering and exiting from the perimeter. This strategy allows the reduction of the volume of traffic in these streets, thus regaining a large amount of thoroughfare that can be dedicated to pedestrians – for leisure, walking, playing and so on. And when this kind of urban arrangement is applied to very neat, disciplined areas, such as the Ensanche Cerdá grid, it is possible to repurpose the old intersections into public squares as a result of the emptying of the streets of traffic, in this case, via the octagon formed by the streets and building façades.

To address the problems stemming from mass tourism and gentrification, various instruments for deterring people from abandoning their neighboroods are now been applied. To this end the ongoing debate and the work on the transformation of the Rambla do not just touch on questions about the physical appearance of places, but on also socio-economic and socio-cultural considerations, with the aim of coming up with solutions that embrace the reappropriation of public spaces and of the residential and commercial fabric in order to make the inhabitants of a district feel more settled and rooted.

Whilst being perfectly aware that great urban transformations today carry the risk of causing the expulsion of residents, in designing the conversion of the old Prisión Modelo, (which we would like to set as an example of the regeneration process of a large-scale architectural complex), we have devoted a substantial part of it to public housing, while other spaces will accommodate local services and facilities. Housing is our greatest concern, but also urban renewal, and therefore we are planning operations to counter the degradation of marginal districts like Can Peguera, where the character of an urban community that views the street as a collective space has still been kept alive. We are working, therefore, to be able to start on the technical implementation of the projects, but bearing in mind particularly the need to assure the quality of everyday life.

The key lies in managing to share these decisions on urban transformation, which should be viewed in the light of the individual freedom of all male and female citizens, in order to guarantee their active involvement, in line with extremely open-minded strategies that give consideration to gender issues and the more vulnerable social groups. A win-win situation for all!

Barcelona beyond the model

Alessandro Scarnato*

Architecture has always played a seminal role in Barcelona's urban planning practices and the much fêted "Barcelona Model" aroused keen interest worldwide mostly because of the quality and quantity of works constructed, rather than the theoretical and technical premises behind them.

The Barcelona of the Olympics – courageous, experimental, even vehement in its urban development planning, and uninhibited in its architecture – is still visible in many constructions scattered throughout the city, from the great hub of the ring-road to the great landmarks by Foster, Isozaki or Calatrava, as well as in the numerous regenerated public spaces – all reflected to some extent in the resounding tourist success of today.

That first fruitful season evolving from the eighties to the beginning of the new century was followed by a period of municipal indulgence towards the glamorous archistars, and this in turn, also on account of the rise of a new school of technicians conscious of social complexities, prompted a harsh volte-face; severe criticism was addressed against the architectural narcissism of the Olympic city, stigmatized as a showcase for global investment rather than as a place for living in.

In 2011, the Smart City theories, represented locally by the Metapolis group, were introduced into the city's urban planning with the Christian Democrat Council which, after over thirty years, managed to seize the City Hall from the Socialist Administration. The coincidental effectiveness of the Smart approach, which was not so interested in the creation of specific works, combined with the harsh effects of the 2008 economic crisis, paradoxically opened a window of practical possibilities for a generation of architects finally liberated from both the cumbersome example of the hero-maestros of the Olympic Barcelona times, and from the implicit Barcelona imperative to produce "designer architecture".

Thus we had a wide-ranging patchwork of over 8,000 professionals operating in the city who were able to play with various approaches towards the role of architectural designer, interpreted from one extreme, as the artist endowed with his own aesthetic ideal, and from the other – as the quiet technician concerned with concrete social or commercial needs.

Some professional studios add civic commitment to entrepreneurial endeavour, developing projects to be executed (also physically) by the residents. In the work of cooperatives like *La Col*, *El Globus Vermell* or *Raons Públiques*, the profile of the architect fades away almost completely and is diluted with the other players in the building process. Though not abandoning the *auteur* aspect of architecture, firms like Harquitectes, Vora or Ravetllat Ribas acknowledge the constructive mission of the profession, identifying the mainspring of their work in materiality and typological reflection. Other names, like Arquitectura-G, MAIO, SUMO Arquitectes or Mesura, carry out research in which the contribution of the design architect is strictly func-

* Architect PhD, Adjunct Professor of the History of Architecture at the Polytechnic University of Catalonia, author of the volume *Top Model Barcelona, 1979-2011, un racconto urbano tra architettura, politica e società* (Altralinea edizioni, Florence, 2015)

tional to the definition of a group operational approach. These are studios that rework the recent past, distilling it through the filter of a technical and communicative awareness deriving from permanent contact with the international scene. The big names of the eighties and nineties (some of whom are still active, like MBM, Llinàs, Càceres or Mateo) often viewed the architect as an interpreter, if not originator, of the planning project. Among those who are continuing such an approach we might place b720 Fermín Vázquez, Prats & Flores, Garcès-De Seta-Bonet or BAAS-Jordi Badia. A continuity that was expressed according to an expanded, refreshed and even pragmatist compositional vision in works that were, nevertheless, not deprived of creative lyricism.

If we shift our gaze from the actual concrete works to the disciplinary debate, the Barcelona scene at the moment is distinguished by a renewed vitality, to which the victory of the alternative left citizen platform *Barcelona en Comú* in the 2015 municipal elections contributed. The new administration rejects policies advocating great public works and infrastructural expansion, preferring to give priority to environmental, economic and social sustainability, to constructional, heritage-based urban regeneration, involving also the participation of citizens. This marks a substantial change for a city that has succeeded in shaking off the chains of the dismal architecture and aggressive urban planning of Franco's times, also thanks to the protagonist role accorded to the figure of the architectural Übermensch. A change, moreover, that has come at a critical moment: the 2017 regional law on architecture was conceived in order to instill disciplinary awareness at all levels of building activity, public and private.

Simultaneously, the historic Architecture School of the Polytechnic is involved in a generational transition complicated by the economic austerity of the crisis. Finally, the arrival of new players on the global scene (clients, businesses, investors and... designers) has made inevitable a drastic rethinking of the meaning of city construction and, again, of the role of the professional in what was the "city of architects", according to the well-known definition by the journalist and author Llàtzer Moix.

Sagrada Familia
Vila Olímpica Towers
PRBB Parc de Recerca Biomèdica de Barcelona

Gas Natural Fenosa
Barceló Raval
W Barcelona

Meliá Barcelona Sky
Oficines Hines 123

Torre Glòries (Torre Agbar)
MediaPro
Diagonal 197
Campus del Poblenou
Museu del Disseny de Barcelona
Universitat Pompeu Fabra

Strategies for visiting Barcelona

To visit Barcelona well, it is best to plan at least five or six days. Four itineraries have been proposed in this guide, and all can be followed on foot or by subway. The shortest itinerary is the first, and focuses on the old centre of the city, which can be seen in a single day. The Medieval Gothic buildings which are particularly important in this area have not been included in the guide, so we advise visitors to refer to specific guides for these architectural examples.

Itinerary A / Ciutat Vella
This route includes several significant buildings, mainly in the old city dating before the 19th century. The choices focus almost exclusively on contemporary architecture and the redevelopment or restoration of old buildings. In particular, from the 1980s to the present day, the Ciutat Vella has been the centre of numerous projects, including urban planning, which have made the area one of the most dynamic in the city. The itinerary begins on the east side with the **Mercat de Sant Antoni/01**, crosses the Raval quarter, now home to several important contemporary art and culture museums like the **MACBA**, the **CCCB/07**, the **Filmoteca de Catalunya/04**, to continue to the west through the Ribera and Born quarters, with the two important markets of **Santa Caterina/08** and **Born/09**, before reaching the seafront, at Barceloneta, terminating at the **W Barcelona/13**.

Itinerary B / Poblenou
This itinerary includes the east side of the city, encompassing the Poblenou quarter, the historical expansion of the initial urban centre, and home to important industrial factories from the early 19th century. The route includes some visits in the **Vila Olímpica/15**, an urban area particularly important in the contemporary history of Barcelona, transformed for the 1992 Olympic Games. The route continues further east, from Plaça de les Glòries Catalanes as far as the zone which hosted the Forum of Cultures in 2004.
Starting at **Torre Agbar/22**, the route continues along the length of Avinguda Diagonal, with a number of new buildings, mainly office blocks, which form a faceted wall of striking high-tech architecture, including the **Diagonal 197/23** and **MediaPro/24**. Former industrial plants were the foundation for the construction of the **Poblenou Campus/26** and the **Museu Can Framis/29**. In the zone closer to the seafront, among the buildings constructed for the Forum of Cultures, the guide includes the **CCIB Centre de Convencions Internacionals de Barcelona/36** and the **Museu de Ciències Naturals de Barcelona/37**.

Itinerary C / Montjuïc – Llobregat

This itinerary covers the western side of the city from the Montjuïc hill to the Llobregat river and includes the Zona Franca and the Porta Fira Trade Fair. The Montjuïc area is above all linked with the Universal Exposition of 1929, and the very famous **German Pavilion/41** by Mies van der Rohe, and the 1992 Olympic Games, which led to the expansion of the sports facilities and the creation of the **Torre de Comunicacions de Montjuïc/45** by Santiago Calatrava. Further along the Avinguda de la Gran Via is the **Ciutat de la Justícia/48** and the Plaça d'Europa with the **Torres Porta Fira/52**. The Zona Franca, flanked by the new subway line with the interesting **Metro L9 stations/51**, houses the **Parc Logístic/53** area, one of the most important service industries in the country for international goods flow that will be linked with the airport and the high speed railway line through the new subway lines.

Itinerary D / Eixample – Gràcia – Sants – Sarrià

This final itinerary focuses on the most significant architecture in the northern area of the city. It includes the interesting restoration and redevelopment plan of the **Centre Cívic Cristalleries Planell/61**, and the **Mercat del Ninot/64**. It also focuses on some of the most important modernist buildings in the Eixample, following the application of the Cerdà Plan (1859). Among the buildings are works by the undisputed Catalan master of Modernism, Antoni Gaudí. As well as the **Sagrada Familia/69** and **Park Güell/75**, we have also selected some residential blocks: **Casa Milà "La Pedrera", Casa Batlló and Casa Vincens/67**, that were recently restored. The 1992 Olympic Games also left their mark in this area with the **Torre de Collserola/82**, designed by Norman Foster, which dominates the Barcelona urban landscape with its 288 metre tower on top of the Tibidabo Hill.

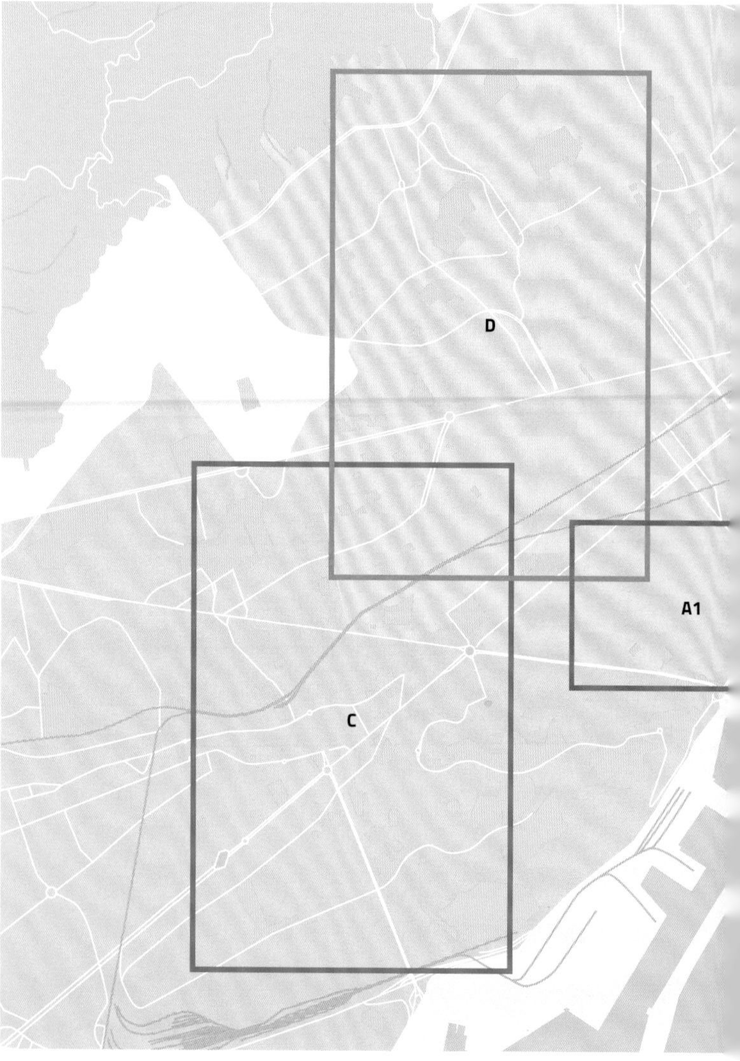
D
A1
C

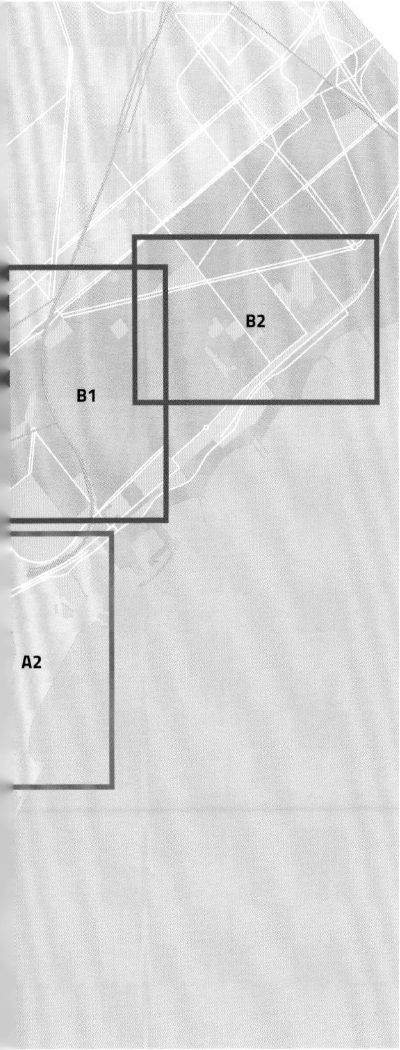

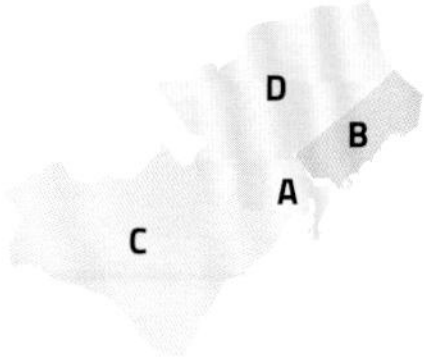

Routes

A. Ciutat Vella
B. Poblenou
C. Montjuïc – Llobregat
D. Eixample – Gràcia – Sants – Sarrià

0 m
100 m
250 m
Universitat
Carrer de Pelai
Carrer dels Tallers
La Rambla
C. de Torres i Amat
Teatre Goya
07
CCCB
MACBA
Ronda de Sant Antoni
Carrer de Sepúlveda
Gran Via de les Corts Catalanes
Carrer de Casanova
Ptge. de Valeri Serra
C. de Muntaner
Alkimia
Fàbrica Moritz Barcelona
Carrer de Villarroel
Carrer del Lleó
Carrer d'Elisabets
Dos Palillos
C. d'en Xuclà
Hotel 1898
Teatre Poliorama
Plaça de les Caramelles
C. del Pintor Fortuny
Carrer del Carme
Hotel Curious
Carrer de la Lluna
Carrer de Floridablanca
Carrer de Sant Gil
Carrer de la Riera Alta
C. de les Egipcíaques
Antic Hospital de la Santa Creu
Jardins de Rubió i Lluch
06
Sant Antoni
Carrer Comte d'Urgell
Carrer de Tamarit
C. de Sant Antoni Abat
01
Cera 23
05
Barceló Raval
Rambla del Raval
04
Carrer de l'Aurora
Carrer de Manso
02
C. de la Reina Amàlia
Carrer de la Riereta
C. de Sant Oleguer
Carrer del Parlament
Carrer del Comte Borrell
Carrer de Viladomat
Plaça de Josep M. Folch i Torres
Ronda de Sant Pau
Carrer de les Carretes
Carrer de Sant Pau
Carrer de les Tàpies
Sant Pau del Camp
C. d'Aldana
Poble Sec
Av. del Paral·lel
Teatre Condal
El Molino
Teatre Victòria
Paral·lel
Teatre Apolo
Carrer de Radas
Carrer de Blai
C. de Margarit
C. de Tapioles
C. de Salvà
C. de Vila i Vilà
7
8
J
K

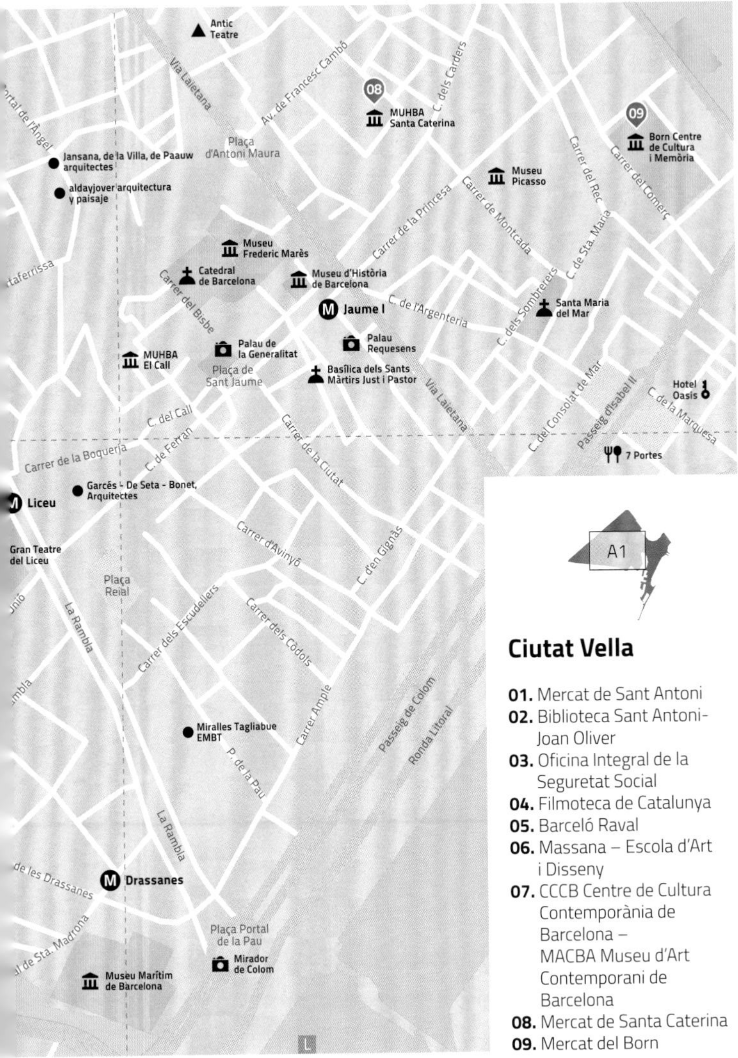

Ciutat Vella

01. Mercat de Sant Antoni
02. Biblioteca Sant Antoni-Joan Oliver
03. Oficina Integral de la Seguretat Social
04. Filmoteca de Catalunya
05. Barceló Raval
06. Massana – Escola d'Art i Disseny
07. CCCB Centre de Cultura Contemporània de Barcelona – MACBA Museu d'Art Contemporani de Barcelona
08. Mercat de Santa Caterina
09. Mercat del Born

M
L
7
8
Carrer de Trelawny
10
Passeig Marítim
Hospital del Mar
Carrer del Gas
Parc de la Barceloneta
Passeig Marítim
Passeig de Circumval·lació
Carrer del Dr. Aiguader
Ronda Litoral
Passeig de S. Papasseit
Plaça de la Maquinista
Plaça d'Antoni Genescà i Coromines
11
Plaça del Gas
Carrer Cermeño
Carrer d'Andrea Dòria
Carrer de la Vila Joiosa
Carrer de F. Rubianes
Parc Zoològic Acuarama
Carrer del Dr. Aiguader
Cova Fumada
Plaça del Poeta Boscà
C. de l'Atlàntida
Carrer de la Maquinista
Carrer de Balboa
Carrer de Ginebra
Carrer del Mar
Carrer de Sant
Passeig Joan de Borbó
12
Estació de França
Barceloneta
Plaça de Pau Vila
Passeig de Picasso
Av. del Marquès de l'Argentera
Born Centre de Cultura i Memòria
09
Hotel Oasis
C. de la Marquesa
7 Portes
Carrer del Comerç
Carrer del Rec
C. de Sta. Maria
Santa Maria del Mar
C. del Consolat de Mar
Passeig d'Isabel II
C. dels Sombrerers
Museu Picasso
Carrer de la Princesa
Via Laietana
C. de la Fusteria
Passeig de Colom
Ronda Litoral
Carrer de l'Ictín

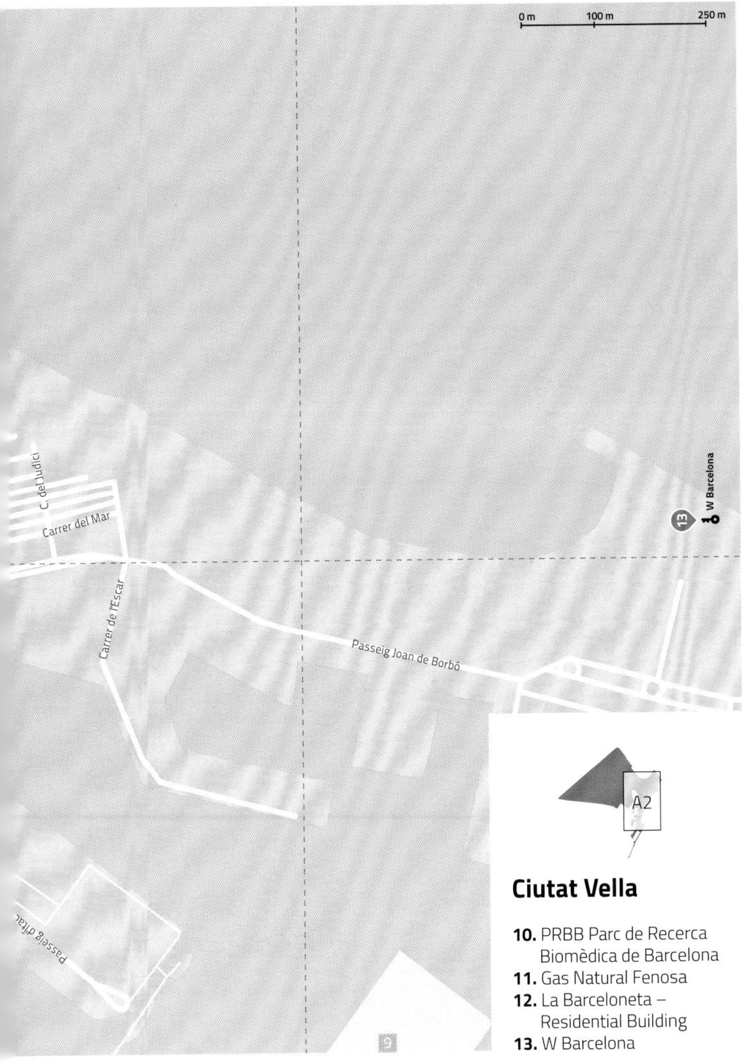

Ciutat Vella

10. PRBB Parc de Recerca Biomèdica de Barcelona
11. Gas Natural Fenosa
12. La Barceloneta – Residential Building
13. W Barcelona

01. Mercat de Sant Antoni

Carrer del Comte Urgell, 1
08011, Barcelona

Mon - Sat / 8 am - 8 pm
Sun / closed

+34 93 426 35 21
info@mercatdesantantoni.com
www.mercatdesantantoni.com

L2 > Sant Antoni

Barcelona has a long tradition of covered public markets which have always represented a fundamental urban element and an important collective space for the population working there and buying their daily food products.
Among the most important and emblematic iron and glass markets is that of Sant Antoni (Antoni Rovira i Trias, Josep Maria Cornet i Mas, 1882) and its layout with four wings that meet in a central space covered by an octagonal roof. It covers an entire block and is a main feature in the Cerdà urban plan just where it meets with the old city.
The Sant Antoni market reconstruction was awarded to the architects Ravetllat Ribas who, to recover enough space for the new market structure, eliminated all the internal elements inside the iron and glass shell, whose decorative and structural details were carefully restored (like the enamelled ceramic roof and central dome covered in terracotta tiles). Underneath the traditional market that sells fresh food and clothes, there is a large supermarket, a gymnasium, neighbourhood services and parking. During the excavations, the archaeological remains of the Bastion of Sant Antoni, part of the ancient walls of the 17th century, were discovered and incorporated as a large public hall in the underground floor.

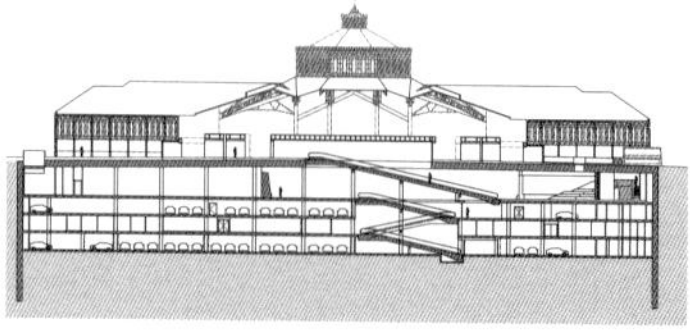

architects
Ravetllat Ribas arquitectes

type
public market - retail

construction
2009 - 2018 (renovation)

02. Biblioteca Sant Antoni-Joan Oliver

Carrer del Comte Borrell, 44-46
08015, Barcelona

25 June - 25 September
Mon, Fri / 4 pm - 8.30 pm
Tue, Thu / 10 am - 2 pm, 4 pm - 8.30 pm
Wed / 10 am - 8.30 pm
Sat / closed
25 September - 25 June
Mon, Fri / 4 pm - 8.30 pm
Tue, Thu / 10 am - 2 pm, 4 pm - 8.30 pm
Wed / 10 am - 8.30 pm
Sat / 10 am - 2 pm

+34 93 329 72 16

L2 > Sant Antoni
L3 > Poble Sec

This building is a functional blend (library, social space for the elderly, and children's play park) which provides dynamic impact by recovering the internal space of an urban block as a public space.
The façade on the street resembles a large gate on an urban scale. The two side blocks are attached to the blind walls of adjacent apartment buildings and house the stairs and elevators. The first floor central block contains the reading areas featuring playful tiered seating between glass walls to create visual tension with the courtyard below, enclosed within the urban block.
The irregular lots that surround the internal courtyard are harmonised through the use of a continuous plinth around the perimeter, built to single floor height, partly composed of usable space, and partly forming separation and boundary walls. The building also houses a retirement home, and a translucent space with an external portico that overlooks a shady enclosed garden, equipped as a children's playground.
Irregular dark vertical metal slats create a sun screen, and when used as cladding give the whole building a unified effect.

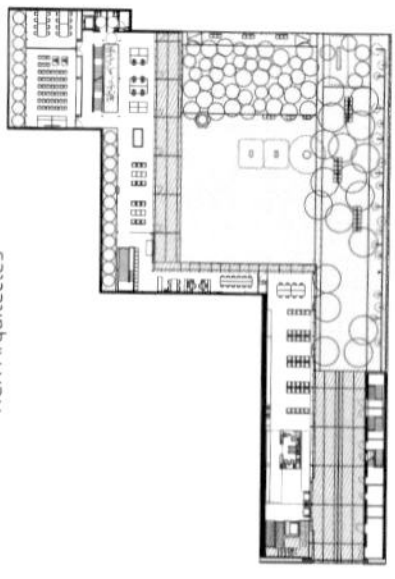

architects
RCR Arquitectes

type
library

construction
2005 - 2007

03. Oficina Integral de la Seguretat Social

Carrer de l'Arc del Teatre, 63
08001, Barcelona

Mon - Fri / 9 am - 2 pm
Sat - Sun / closed

+34 93 327 15 50

www.seg-social.es

L3 > Drassanes

The Social Security Administration Building occupies the southern part of the Raval quarter, previously considered a marginal area, but that has recently undergone considerable urban redevelopment. Integrating this structure within the urban plan on the sites of former buildings influenced the size and shape of the project. Horizontally, the building is divided into three sections which rotate slightly in relation to one another. The ground floor follows the geometrical shape of the site, the second (first to fourth floors) is aligned with the street, Carrer de l'Om, creating a wide portico that protects the entrance to the building. The third section (fifth and sixth floors) is rotated again to realign it with the ground floor. As well as providing a sense of movement, with interesting chiaroscuro effects on the façades, positioning the sections in different directions made it possible to create a terrace accessed from the fifth floor. The façades are clad with a continuous shell of horizontal aluminium slats as protection from direct sunlight. The structural columns around the façades provide open internal space with more versatile layout possibilities. A public space with a paved square and planted trees surrounds the building.

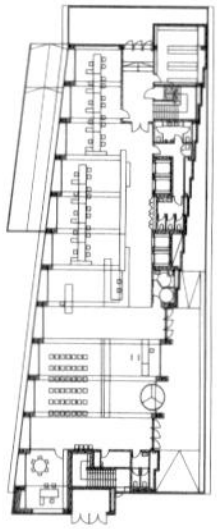

architects
BCQ arquitectura barcelona

type
offices

construction
2009 - 2011

04. Filmoteca de Catalunya

Plaça de Salvador Seguí, 1-9
08001, Barcelona

open to the public

+34 93 567 10 70
filmoteca.cultura@gencat.cat
www.filmoteca.cat

L3 > Liceu

The Filmoteca is located in the historic Raval quarter, an area that has recently undergone considerable transformation, while maintaining its densely popular character as a port neighbourhood. The location determined the size and shape of the building. The scale is linked with its unusual proportions, and the new square that was created in front of the building has brought an open airy atmosphere to the area. The projection rooms were created underground to avoid a heavy effect, and the transparent ground floor space provides an easy-flowing passage between the square and the streets to the rear.

The building has a bare unclad structure. The exposed concrete façades, with very different textures, are a reference to the deteriorated walls in the surrounding neighbourhood. The structural concept was based on the building's requirements: it is composed of two rectangular blocks, one of which is built completely underground. The other rises above the square, and houses the work spaces. The façades along the length of the building define the construction above ground, while the transversal façades form a series of projecting elements.

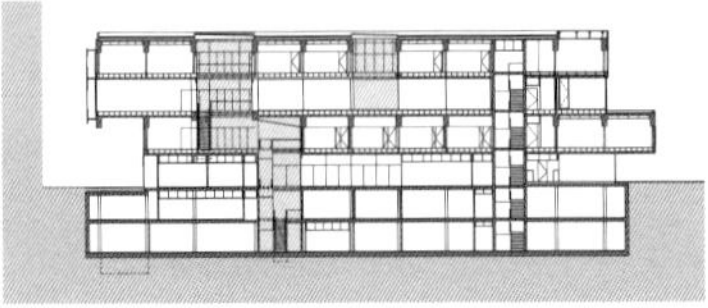

© Adrià Goula

architects
Mateo Arquitectura

type
cinema, museum

construction
2011

05. Barceló Raval

Rambla del Raval, 17-21

08001, Barcelona

open to the public

+34 93 320 14 90
raval@barcelo.com
www.barcelo.com

L3 > Liceu

La Rambla del Raval (Pere Cabrera, Jaume Artigues, 1998), was inaugurated in 2000; the wide pedestrian avenue paved in concrete and granite is planted with palm trees and flower beds along the whole length. It is bordered by two streets for vehicle traffic with wide tree-lined pavements. This large-scale intervention covers an area 58 metres wide by 317 metres long, made possible by the demolition of five city blocks. In 2007, it was decided to demolish a further block close to the Rambla del Raval, la Illa Robadors, renowned for its unsavoury reputation and illegal activities. The firm, MBM Arquitectes (at the time lead by Josep Martorell, Oriol Bohigas, David Mackay), was commissioned to draw up the urban project and design a residential building. The hotel Barceló Raval was inaugurated in 2008: an eleven story cylinder clad with a translucent "skin" that lights up at night like a giant lamp. The height and shape of this unusual hotel have made it an iconic feature in harmony with the surrounding cityscape, part of an ongoing urban renewal project.

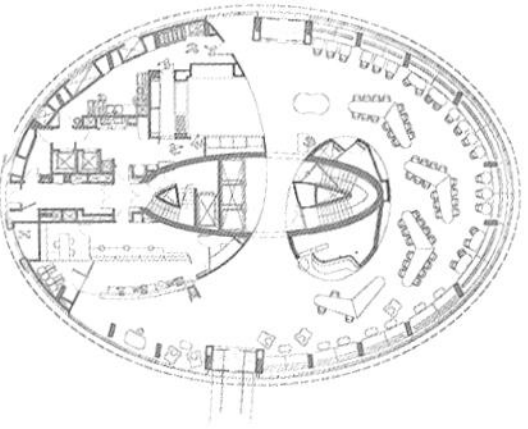

© CMV Architects

architects
CMV Architects

type
hotel

construction
2004 - 2008

06. Massana – Escola d'Art i Disseny

Plaça Gardunya, 9
08001, Barcelona

open to the public

+34 934 42 20 00

www.escolamassana.cat

L3 > Liceu

Located behind the Boqueria market, the Massana centre is the faculty for university courses in visual arts and design. The project is part of a complex urban renewal intervention that also included the recovery of an adjacent open space (Plaça Gardunya), a new residential building, and the redesigning of the rear façade of the Boqueria market.
The L-shaped layout of the building hinges around a full-height central atrium, lit from above and crossed by walkways at various levels. Terraces and loggias at each end of the circulation galleries overlook the square to create a connection with the city.
The various fragmented façades create a contrast with their adjacent elements. They are clad in large-scale, artisanally produced, ceramic elements in two versions: red ceramic sun screen slatting facing the square, and grey ceramic for the ventilated façade overlooking the street.
The building aimed at an original design, but without becoming a dominant feature in the square. For this reason, the entrance has been placed to the side of the building for easy access to the future Biblioteca de Catalunya.

© Estudio Carme Pinós

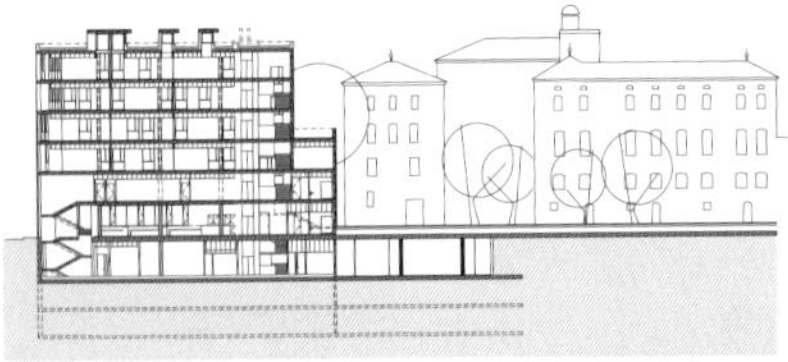

architects
Estudio Carme Pinós

type
school centre

construction
2017

07. CCCB Centre de Cultura Contemporània de Barcelona – MACBA Museu d'Art Contemporani de Barcelona

CCCB
Carrer de Montalegre, 5
08001, Barcelona

Tue - Sun / 11 am - 8 pm
Mon / closed

+34 93 306 41 00

info@cccb.org
www.cccb.org

L1 / L2 > Universitat

Two of the most important museums in the city were created in the northern part of the Raval district in the mid-nineties: the MACBA Museu d'Art Contemporani de Barcelona and the CCCB Centre de Cultura Contemporània de Barcelona. They were constructed in the area formerly occupied by the Caritat convent complex, partly fallen into disrepair in the 1950s. The Pla Especial de Reforma Interior (PERI) plan, of 1985, had identified a large number of unused public buildings in bad condition, including the Casa de la Caritat, the Casa de la Misericòrdia and the convent complex of dels Àngels. The PERI re-proposed a previous urban project for the two convent complexes and the adjacent church, that had been designed in 1981 by the architects, Lluís Clotet and Óscar Tusquets, entitled "Del Liceu al Seminari". The project envisaged a route running parallel to les Rambles, from the Liceu theatre to Plaça de la Universitat, created by connecting the former convent buildings and giving them a new cultural purpose. The Pla de Museus project, of 1984, and the successive urban development plan for the Casa de la Caritat destined the buildings for museum and exhibition space to "recover and revitalise an important area of the Raval district". The CCCB (Albert Viaplana, estudio Viaplana/Piñón) and the MACBA (Richard Meier & Partners), were inaugurated in 1994 and

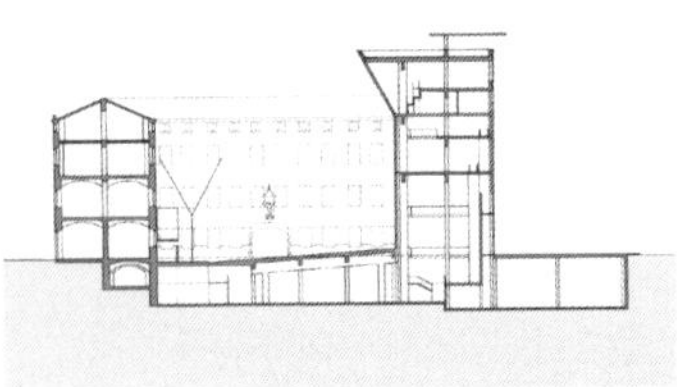

© David Viaplana Canudas

architects
Viaplana/Piñón

type
multi-purpose
exhibition space

construction
1994

MACBA
Plaça dels Àngels, 1
08001, Barcellona

Summer / Mon, Wed - Fri /
11 am - 8 pm
Mon, Wed - Fri /
11 am - 7.30 pm
Sat / 10 am - 8 pm
Sun and Holidays /
10 am - 3 pm
Tue / closed

+34 93 481 33 68

www.macba.cat

L1 / L2 > Universitat

1995, while, directly opposite, the old convent of dels Àngels became the FAD, Foment de les Arts Decoratives (Lluís Clotet, Ignacio Paricio, Carles Díaz). The space that was occupied by FAD, it's now occupied by exhibitions and activities of the MACBA, a study center and a library. Now some of the city's most important cultural buildings overlook the new Plaça dels Àngels, which has housed the Centre d'Estudis i Recursos Culturals (CERC) since 1986. From the square, a route cuts through the white modernist Meier museum to reach another public space, Plaça de Joan Coromines, and from here, it forms a single complex of open spaces through to the Pati de les Dones, where the glass façade of the CCCB slopes from the roof to reflect the urban landscape inside the enclosed courtyard. Barcelona finally achieved its cultural "cluster": the urban development plan, urban project, and the architectural and cultural project were interwoven, and like Paris, the city obtained its Pompidou Center, even before Bilbao built its Guggenheim. MACBA houses a collection of contemporary international art, and holds interesting temporary exhibitions, while the CCCB is an extremely vibrant research and diffusion centre focussed on the city, with a fine library and study rooms.

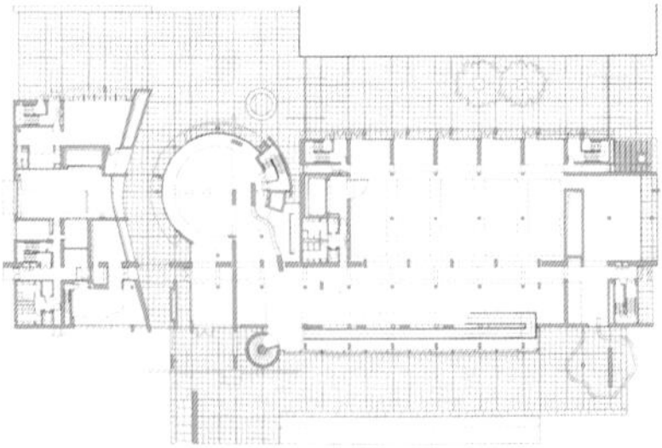

© Courtesy Richard Meier & Partners Architects

architects
Richard Meier &
Partners Architects

type
museum

construction
1987 - 1995

08. Mercat de Santa Caterina

Avinguda de Francesc Cambó, 16
08003, Barcelona

Mon, Wed, Sat /
7.30 am - 3.30 pm
Tue, Thu, Fri /
7.30 am - 8.30 pm

+34 93 319 57 40
info@mercatsantacaterina.cat
www.mercatsantacaterina.com

L4 > Jaume I

The Santa Caterina market, inaugurated in 1848, was the first covered market in Barcelona. The reconstruction project also includes the surrounding urban fabric in order to improve the quality of the public spaces.
The new intervention was aimed at "mixing and blending" with the original structure (which preserved the side walls and portico façade). It features a remarkable new roof that extends beyond the perimeter of the original structure into the adjacent square. Clad externally with a mosaic of enamelled ceramic tiles representing a multi-coloured sea of fruit and vegetables, the roof becomes the main feature of the building with a homage to Gaudí.
The structure is quite complex, based on a series of irregular wooden vaulted ceilings set on steel beams of various sizes, mounted in different directions, and in turn, supported by concrete pillars.
Miralles and Tagliabue conceived the building as a huge tent, inside which the market stalls have been arranged without any specific order, just like traditional rural markets.
Miralles died before the construction was completed.

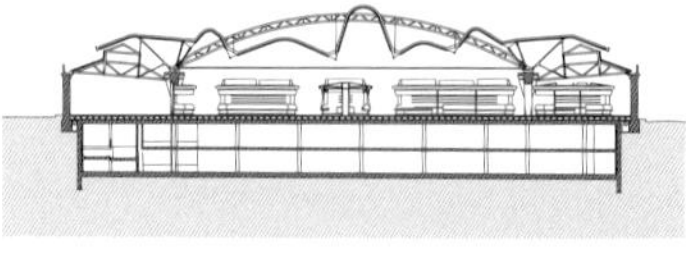

architects	type	construction
Miralles Tagliabue EMBT	retail	2005

09. Mercat del Born

Plaça Comercial, 12
08003, Barcelona

Mon - Sat / 8 am - 8.30 pm
Sun / closed

+34 93 256 68 51

elbornculturaimemoria.
barcelona.cat

L4 > Barceloneta

The old Mercat del Born (Antoni Rovira i Trias, 1873), with its characteristic iron and glass structure, traditionally a local meeting place as well as a food market, was recently converted to create the Born cultural centre, a public space and museum, where visitors can view the remains of the ancient La Ribera quarter (project by Enric Sòria and Rafael de Càceres, 2013). The Vora architectural firm (Pere Buil and Toni Riba) was responsible for the urban development of the Plaça Comercial area that surrounds the market. They designed the pedestrian streets and urban furnishing, connecting the area directly with the near-by Ciutadella Park. The paving was designed to retrace the location of the ancient buildings destroyed by Philip V of Spain to build the Ciutadella fortress following the Spanish War of Succession (1714). The paving in granite cobblestones (mainly recovered from former existing streets and reused) changes colour to form a kind of weave or tattoo that traces and provides an identity in the main area of the Plaça Comercial. The combined market and surrounding open squares pay homage to local history and Catalan culture as well as providing a new public space for the city.

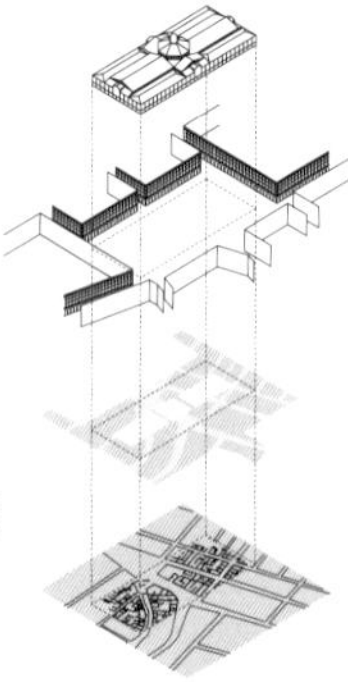

© Vora

architects
Antoni Rovira i Trias /
Vora (external arrangement)

type
retail

construction
1873 / 2013
(external arrangement)

10. PRBB Parc de Recerca Biomèdica de Barcelona

Carrer del Dr. Aiguader, 88
08003, Barcelona

Mon - Fri / 8 am - 6 pm
Sat - Sun / closed

+34 93 316 00 00
comunicacio@prbb.org
www.prbb.org

L4 > Ciutadella | Vila Olímpica

The Parc de Recerca Biomèdica de Barcelona (PRBB) is set on the Passeig Marítim in Barceloneta, close to the sea, and adjacent to the Hospital del Mar (also designed by Brullet-de Luna i Associats + PINEARQ). Along with the university complexes of Universitat Pompeu Fabra and Universitat Autònoma de Barcelona, these buildings form a single compound incorporating health care, education, and research.
Set on a concrete platform, this large-scale structure (about 35,000 square metres) has a truncated conical shape cut diagonally, with an elliptical base, and slopes down towards the sea.
The various internal spaces are arranged around a large central courtyard which houses the auditorium, to provide a magnificent view of the sea. The façades are clad in red cedar brise-soleil slats that help lighten the effect of the massive structure. Solar panels on the roof produce hot water and electricity.

© Brullet-de Luna i Associats + PINEARQ

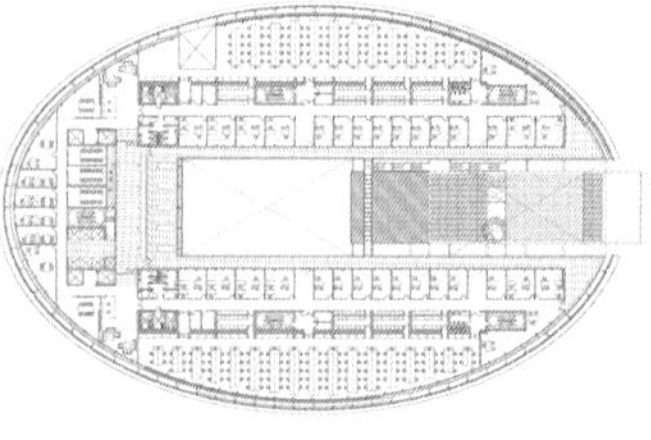

architects
Brullet-de Luna i
Associats + PINEARQ

type
research centre

construction
2001 - 2006

11. Gas Natural Fenosa

Plaça del Gas & C / Doctor Aiguader, 1
08003, Barcelona

external viewing only

L4 > Barceloneta

The new Gas Natural headquarters is a 22-storey tower, 86 metres high, located in Barceloneta. Its design demonstrates a clear desire for integration with the surrounding neighbourhood where fishermans' houses coexist alongside 5-floor apartment buildings, and with the new skyscrapers that form the urban skyline.
The building echoes traditional vertical office block design, but with strongly contrasting horizontal elements that create a connection with adjacent residential buildings. The most spectacular element is the large projecting block that forms a gateway open towards the Barceloneta district.
Rather than a single building, this seems like a complex of sculptural elements playing against one another, but unified by the glass cladding that wraps the building, to give ever-changing shades of colour. The configuration changes constantly when seen from different directions. The glimmering effect is enhanced by the specifically designed glass cladding with tiny distortions that create reflections "that flicker like gas flames", according to Benedetta Tagliabue. Special attention was paid to the new external spaces.

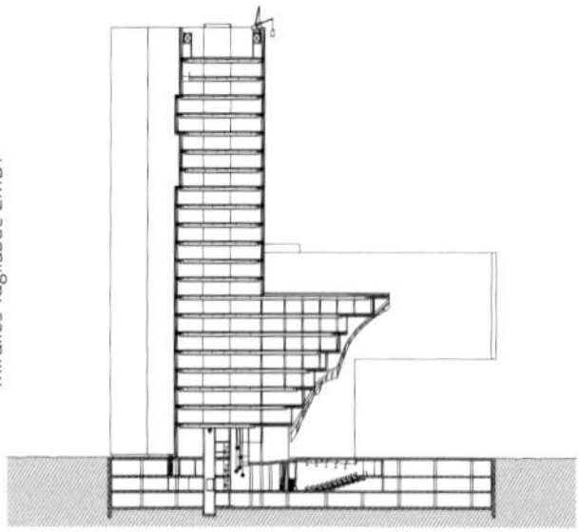

architects
Miralles Tagliabue EMBT

type
offices

construction
2007

12. La Barceloneta – Residential Building

Carrer del Marquès de Sentmenat, 84
08029, Barcelona

external viewing only

L4 > Barceloneta

With this apartment building in Barceloneta, Coderch consolidated his reputation as one of the protagonists of European architecture in the post-war period. The apartment building built in Passeig de Joan de Borbó represents the condominium prototype that Coderch was to apply several times for private housing until the beginning of the seventies. In this case, the building was a public housing project destined for the fishermen of Barceloneta. The design required space for retail shops on the ground floor, and 7 storeys for small apartments. The architect wanted to create movement on the façades and built the external bearing walls with sections at slight angles to form oblique effects. The three open façades are composed of alternating vertical sections clad in brick-red ceramic tiles, and white wooden louvre shutters, all crowned by a projecting roof for shade. The use of shutters with adjustable slats from floor to ceiling became a recurring element in many of Coderch's façades and the style of the Catalan architect was similar to certain projects by his Italian contemporary, Ignazio Gardella, like his Borsalino residential blocks. The apartments are arranged around a compact vertical central core containing the stairways and elevators. The average apartment measures 72 square metres, and there are two per floor. The internal areas with slanting partitions and triangular spaces recall the layouts of "La Pedrera" by Antoni Gaudí.

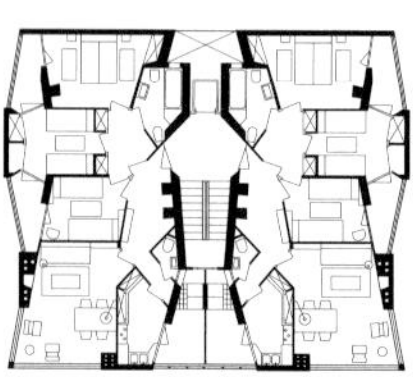

© Archivio Coderch

architects
José Antonio Coderch
de Sentmenat

type
residential

construction
1951

13. W Barcelona

Plaça de la Rosa dels Vents 1 Final, Passeig de Joan de Borbó
08039, Barcelona

open to the public

+34 93 295 28 00

L4 > Barceloneta

The sail-shaped profile of the W Barcelona hotel (also called the Sail Hotel) stands out alongside the Olympic Village Towers to define the new skyline of the Barcelona coast. The hotel is located on the new entrance to the port of Barcelona in the Barceloneta quarter, on 10 hectares of land reclaimed from the sea only a few metres from the coastline, and although criticised by some, it immediately became the new icon of the city open to international tourism. It is a 5 star hotel, 105 metres high, with 26 floors, 480 rooms, 67 suites, a roof bar area, a large health spa, and indoor and outdoor swimming pools. The façade is clad with 15,594 square metres of reflective silver glass designed to make the building blend with the colours of the sea and the sky. The complex includes a large congress centre.

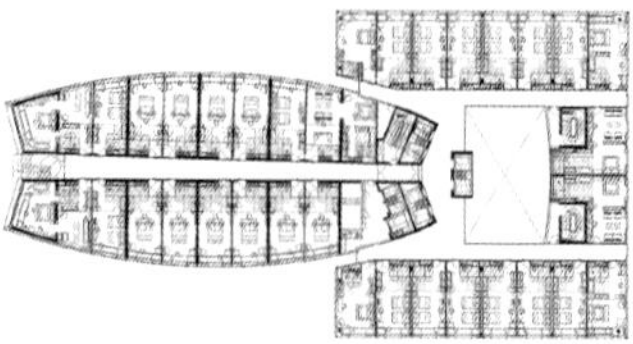

architects
Ricardo Bofill Taller
de Arquitectura

type
hotel

construction
2009

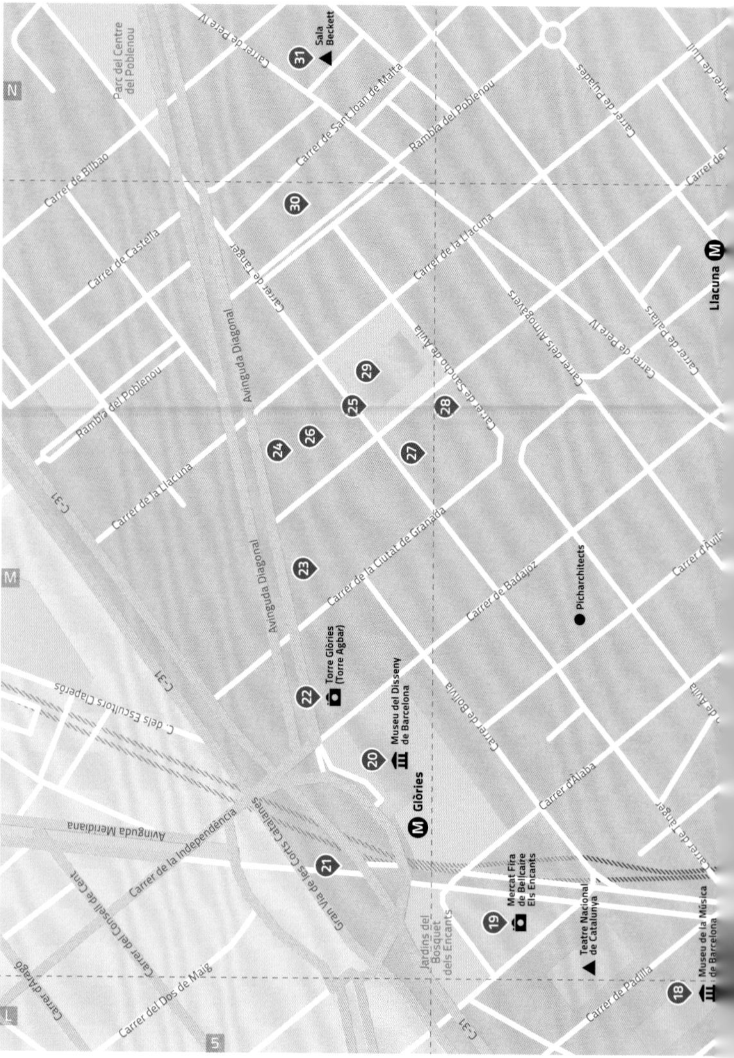
N
M
L
5
Parc del Centre del Poblenou
Carrer de Pere IV
31
Sala Beckett
Carrer de Sant Joan de Malta
Rambla del Poblenou
Carrer de Bilbao
30
Carrer de Castella
Carrer de Tànger
Carrer de la Llacuna
Carrer de Pujades
Carrer dels Almogàvers
Carrer de Pallars
Llacuna
Avinguda Diagonal
29
25
24
26
28
27
Carrer de Sancho de Àvila
C-31
23
Carrer de la Ciutat de Granada
Carrer de Badajoz
Picharchitects
Carrer d'Àvila
Torre Glòries (Torre Agbar)
22
C. dels Escultors Claperós
Museu del Disseny de Barcelona
20
Glòries
Carrer de Bolívia
Carrer d'Àlaba
Avinguda Meridiana
Carrer de la Independència
Gran Via de les Corts Catalanes
21
Mercat Fira de Bellcaire Els Encants
19
Jardins del Bosquet dels Encants
Teatre Nacional de Catalunya
Carrer del Consell de Cent
Carrer d'Aragó
Carrer del Dos de Maig
Carrer de Padilla
18
Museu de la Música de Barcelona

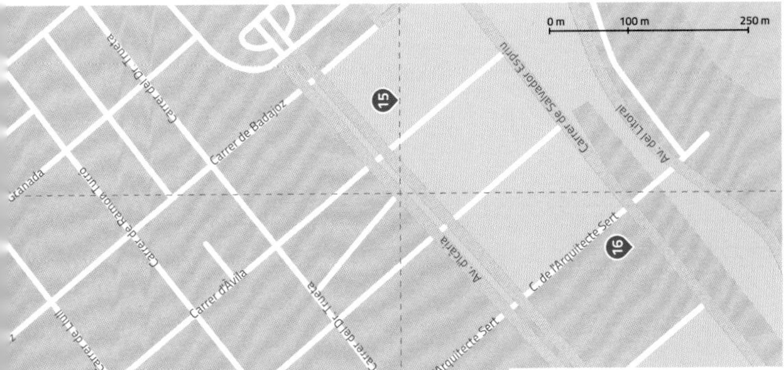

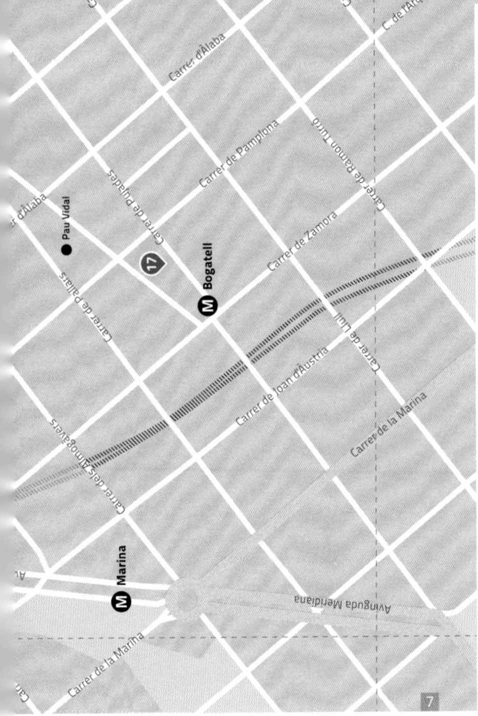

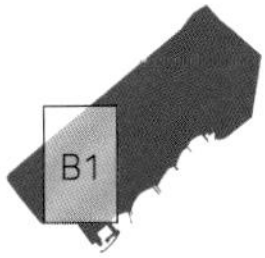

Poblenou

14. Triton Building
15. Vila Olímpica del Poblenou – Residential Complex
16. Agencia Estatal De Meteorología
17. Plug-in
18. Auditori de Barcelona
19. Mercat Fira de Bellcaire Els Encants
20. Museu del Disseny de Barcelona
21. Plaça de les Glòries – Pavilion
22. Torre Glòries (Torre Agbar)
23. Diagonal 197
24. MediaPro
25. Universitat Pompeu Fabra
26. Campus del Poblenou
27. Oficines Indra
28. MediaTIC
29. Museu Can Framis
30. Escola Sant Martí

M
N
5
6
34
33
32
30
31
14
Carrer d'Espronceda
Carrer del Marroc
Carrer de Fluvià
Carrer de la Selva de Mar
Carrer de Veneçuela
Carrer de Bac de Roda
Parc del Centre del Poblenou
Avinguda Diagonal
Camí Antic de València
Carrer de Pallars
Meliá Barcelona Sky
Carrer de Fluvià
Carrer de Lope de Vega
Carrer de Pujades
Carrer de Pere IV
Sala Beckett
Carrer de Bilbao
Jardins de Josep Trueta
Jardins de Gandhi
Carrer de Bac de Ro
Poblenou
Carrer de Pallars
Carrer de Llull
Carrer de Ramon Turró
Carrer d'Espronceda
Carrer de Marià Aguiló
Carrer de Pujades
Carrer de Lope de Vega
Carrer de Bilbao
Travelodge Barcelona Poblenou
Llacuna
Carrer de Llull
Carrer de Ramon Turró
Carrer del Taulat
0 m
100 m
250 m

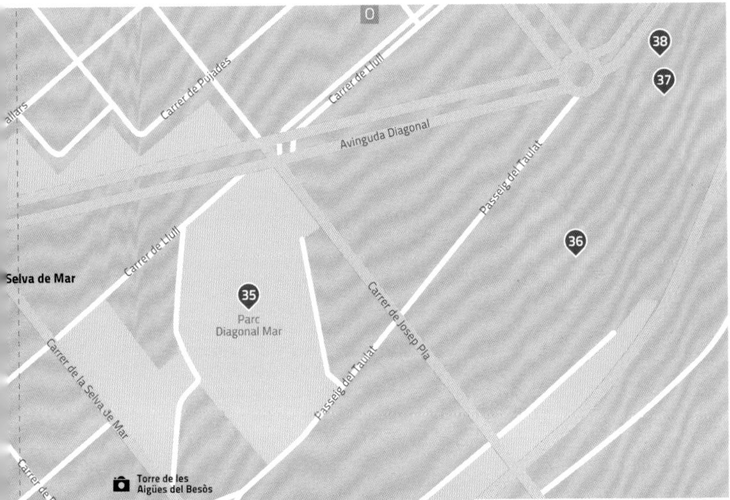

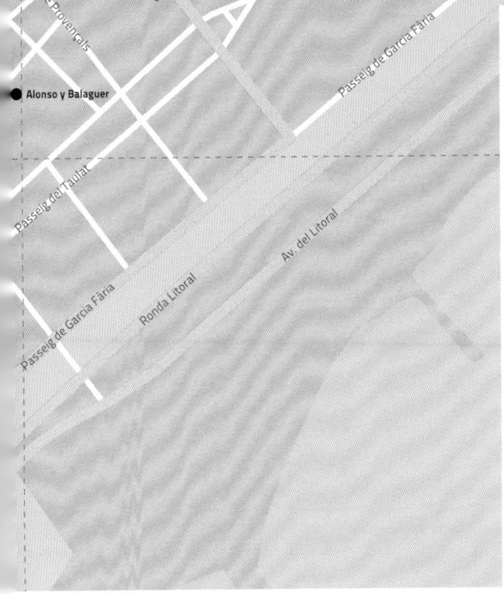

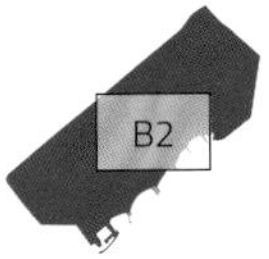

Poblenou

31. Sala Beckett – Obrador Internacional de Dramatúrgia
32. Meliá Barcelona Sky
33. Oficines Hines 123
34. Mental Disabled Residence and Day Centre
35. Parc Diagonal Mar
36. CCIB Centre de Convencions Internacionals de Barcelona
37. Museu de Ciències Naturals de Barcelona
38. Diagonal ZeroZero

14. Triton Building

Passeig Calvell, 45
08005, Barcelona

open to the public

L4 > Poblenou

The Triton Building is a residential complex in the Poblenou district, between the Vila Olímpica and the Diagonal Mar area, near the new beaches and parks created on the seafront. It is composed of 104 rented apartments, retail stores, and underground parking.

The complex has an "E-shaped" layout open towards the coastline so that almost every apartment enjoys sea views. The three blocks that face the sea in a southern direction are clad with aluminium panels in slightly different shades to create attractive light effects. The internal façades overlooking Carrer Perelló are clad in dark ceramic tiles for a more urban look. The roof, which is accessible from all buildings, has an aromatic garden and two swimming pools.

© Saeta Estudi

architects
Saeta Estudi, Lluis
Cantallops, Juan Domingo

type
retail, residential

construction
2010

15. Vila Olímpica del Poblenou – Residential Complex

Plaça de Tirant lo Blanc
08005, Barcelona

external viewing only

L4 > Ciutadella | Vila Olímpica

The Vila Olímpica complex is located in the area of Poblenou where the athletes' village, hotels, offices, and water sports facilities were built for the 1992 Olympic games. Following the games, the athletes' lodgings were converted into normal private apartments. Since the 1990s, the whole Poblenou district as far as its eastern boundaries has been the object of numerous redevelopment projects that have led to the district's complete transformation from an industrial area to a residential and tourist locality as well as home to high tech service industries. The Vila Olímpica plan was organised on three levels: the strategic program, the urban, and the architectural projects. The urban project played a major role in guaranteeing homogeneous coherence among the various components. The general directives for the urban project were interpreted in an original way in the Torres-Lapeña residential complex which occupies two urban blocks in the Cerdá grid plan. The circular complex is composed of two curved blocks plus a terminal structure, all built around a large central square. The smallest, but tallest building, almost oval in shape, forms the closing element of the complex, rather like the bow of a ship. The façades are clad in undulating red brick, and windows have sliding shutters.

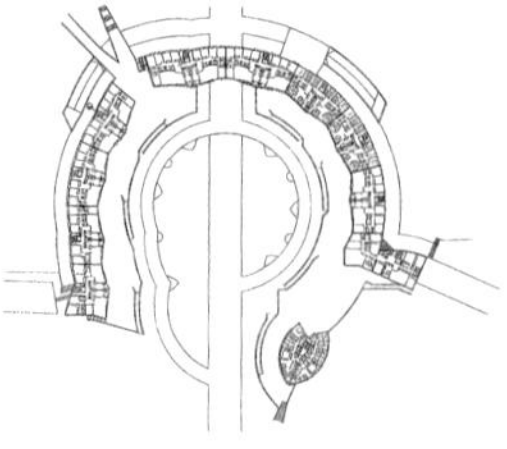

© Martínez Lapeña – Torres Arquitectos

architects
José Antonio Martínez Lapeña
& Elías Torres Architects

type
residential

construction
1992

16. Agencia Estatal De Meteorología

Carrer de l'Arquitecte Sert, 1
08005, Barcelona

Mon - Fri / 9 am - 8 pm
Sat - Sun / closed

+34 93 221 11 47

L4 > Ciutadella | Vila Olímpica

This building is located in the waterfront area of Barcelona and was constructed for the 1992 Olympic Games. It was designed as the headquarters for the weather centre that calculated the forecasts for open-air events and sailing regattas.
The five floors of the building are currently used by the Weather Department and the Port Authorities, which each have separate access.
The base of the concrete building, partly clad in white brick, was excavated on the side facing the sea. Despite its limited size, the building's cylindrical form creates a strong impact in its surroundings. Eight radial openings house small terraces and courtyards, but externally the building seems relatively enclosed. An internal courtyard, 9-metres in diameter, provides natural lighting for all the work spaces. This is the first building designed in Spain by the Portuguese architect.

© Arquitecto Álvaro Siza Vieira

architects
Alvaro Siza

type
infrastructure, offices

construction
1990

17. Plug-in

Carrer de Pujades, 22
08005, Barcelona

external viewing only

L1 > Marina

This complex rises on a site enclosed by three streets: Pujades, Pamplona and Pere IV. The latter, which existed before the Cerdá urban plan, cuts across the Poblenou grid, creating interesting triangular spaces in various points.
The project follows the urban layout aligning the complex with Carrer Pere IV. It is composed of three buildings separated by pedestrian passages, like narrow streets, that provide light to the internal office spaces. The three buildings are also connected by a transversal central passage that houses stairs and elevators.
The geometry of the complex is not in constant alignment and the three buildings have different heights. In a relationship with the old neighbouring industrial building in Carrer de Pamplona, one of the higher buildings has a protruding cantilevered section that seems to act as a partial roof over the old building, and creates a further alignment with the side façade. The complex is built completely on a steel framework.

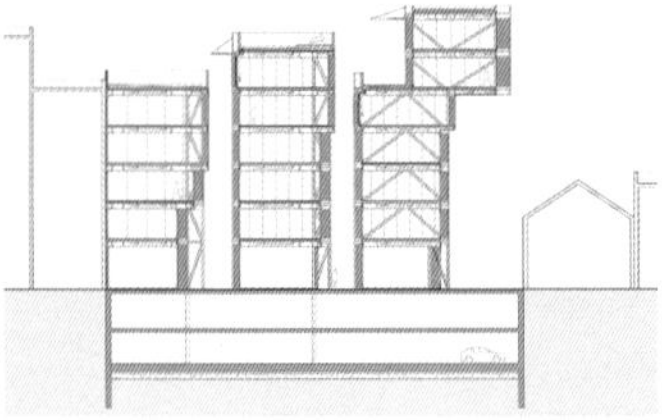

architects
MIAS Arquitectes

type
offices

construction
2008

18. Auditori de Barcelona

Carrer de Lepant, 150
08013, Barcelona

open to the public

+34 93 247 93 00
espais@auditori.cat
www.auditori.cat

L1 > Marina

During the 1990s, the Plaça de les Glòries was redesigned to perform a new urban function. To provide greater potential for this area of the city, especially as a cultural district, several new buildings were constructed in the vicinity: the Teatre Nacional de Catalunya by Ricardo Bofill, 1997, the Arxiu de la Corona d'Aragó (General Archive of the Crown of Aragon) by Roser Amadó, Lluís Domènech, 1993, and the Auditori de Barcelona by Rafael Moneo, 1998.
The auditorium is located on the edge of the Ensanche urban development, where there appears to be a split in the urban fabric. The project concept opted for a building that was independent of the surrounding context, and was placed in the location aligned with the longest side of the block. The building is composed of a single, compact, rectangular volume clad with steel panels set into reinforced concrete frames to produce a regular geometrical effect. They also act as a grid for openings and free standing supports. The external cor-ten steel panels, (with a brick-red finish that changes with the weather) repeat the wooden panels of the interior. The auditorium represents a small musical citadel, housing two concert halls, (seating 2,500 and 700 spectators), a multifunctional space, a Music Museum, and rehearsal space for the Escuela Superior de Música de Catalunya.

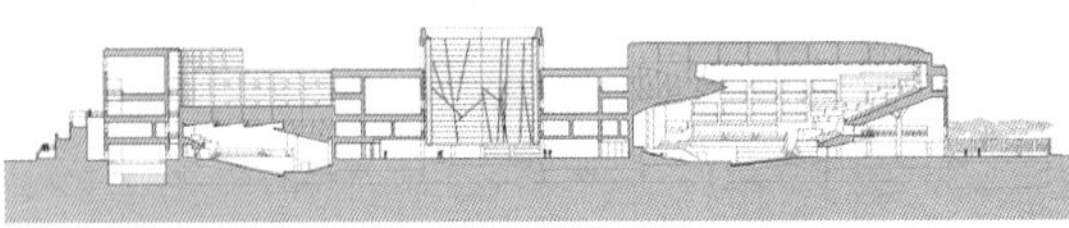

architects
Rafael Moneo

type
theatre

construction
1999

19. Mercat Fira de Bellcaire Els Encants

Carrer de los Castillejos, 158
08013, Barcelona

Mon, Wed, Fri - Sat /
9 am - 8 pm
Tue, Thu, Sun / closed

+34 93 245 22 99
info@encantsbcn.com
www.encantsbcn.com

L1 > Glòries

The old Barcelona Flea market that previously spread out casually on the edge of Plaça de les Glòries for over a hundred years, has been relocated slightly and has become the object of an integrated redesign project by b720 Fermín Vázquez Arquitectos.
The main objective was to maintain the market's open air concept. The restricted size of the new location inspired a project design on various levels. Market stalls are arranged on different floors connected by sloping and partially elevated walkways. The building is sheltered under a large suspended roof almost 25 metres high. It acts as an important reference point while protecting the market stalls, products, and customers from the strong sun. The interior of the roofing is composed of different sections, sloping in various directions and creating fascinating reflections of the flea market below. The building has two underground levels that house the logistics services and public parking.

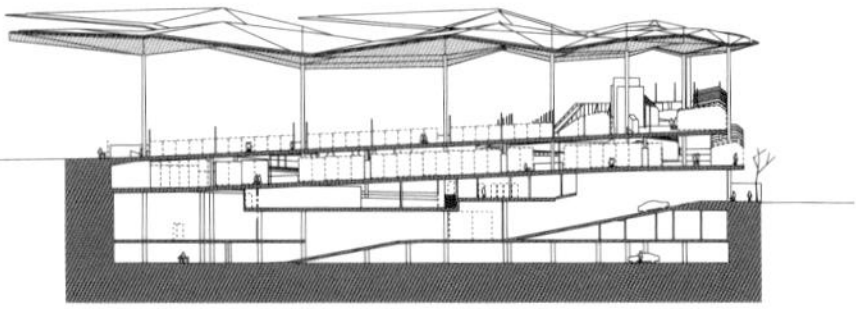

architects
b720 Fermín Vázquez
Arquitectos

type
retail

construction
2013

20. Museu del Disseny de Barcelona

Plaça de les Glòries Catalanes, 37
08018, Barcelona

Tue - Sun / 10 am - 8 pm
Mon / closed

+34 93 256 68 00

museudeldisseny.cat

L1 > Glòries

The new Museu del Disseny de Barcelona, designed by MBM, recently opened its doors to enhance the urban role of Plaça de les Glòries, especially as a cultural centre.
The building has a powerful visual connection with the tall glimmering Torre Agbar, in contrast with its strongly horizontal design and use of aluminium panel cladding. The building is composed of two blocks: an underground section (using the change in levels created by the square), mainly glass-enclosed with views over a large public space partly occupied by a mirror pool. The second section is a 14.5 metre, seven-storey structure with a complex profile whose roof protrudes out over the street like a vast canopy. The museum houses collections of decorative arts, ceramics, fabrics and graphics by the city's main designers. As well as the exhibition spaces, the building has an auditorium, small reception area, public library, educational space, and a café.

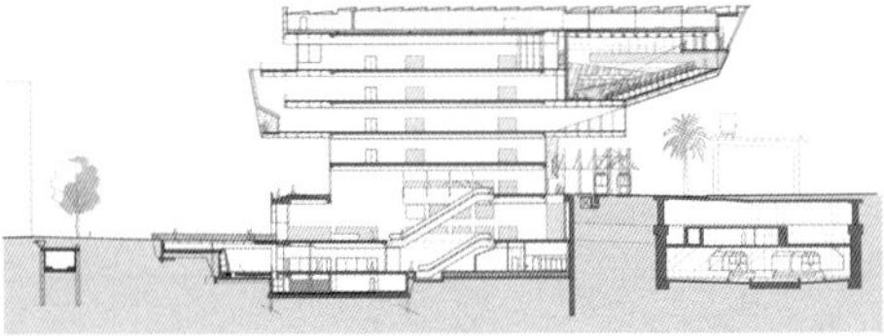

architects
MBM Arquitectes

type
museum

construction
2014

21. Plaça de les Glòries – Pavilion

Plaça de les Glòries Catalanes, 10
08013, Barcelona

open to the public

L1 > Glòries

Located on the waterfront side of the new space created after the demolition of the ring around Plaça de les Glòries, this structure is basically a long pergola, like a temporary open pavilion, designed for use as a public space while awaiting the final configuration of the area according to the CANopen Urbana development plan. Along its total length it offers shade and protection over an open space measuring 700 square metres, creating an urban location that can be adapted for numerous public events. Energetically self-sufficient, the pavilion is composed of seven lightweight modules covered with overhead shade sails fixed with cables. Four of these modules are rain-proof and can be used in wet weather. Other sails are attached to the sides as supports to display information concerning cultural events in the surrounding areas. The vibrant colours of the shade sails were inspired in chromatic terms by the sound of whale songs, arranged and reworked by the cyborg artist Neil Harbisson.

© Calderon-Folch Studio

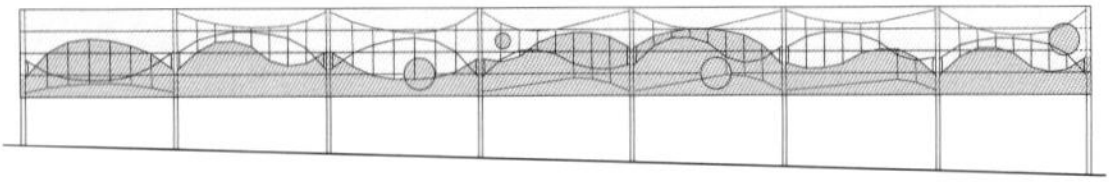

architects
Calderon-Folch Studio,
Pol Sarsanedas

type
multi-purpose space

construction
2014

22. Torre Glòries (Torre Agbar)

Avinguda Diagonal, 211
08018, Barcelona

Mon - Fri / 9 am - 6 pm
Sat - Sun / closed

L1 > Glòries

Constructed between 1999 and 2005, the tower, which originally belonged to Agbar (Sociedad General de Aguas de Barcelona, S.A.) is one of the icons of contemporary Barcelona, rising like a beacon in the new Plaça de les Glòries. This Plaça, which was already an important infrastructural hub in the Cerdá urban development plan, has been redesigned several times since the 1990s. First designed with an elevated, high-speed ring road around a public green park, (Joaquim M. Casamor d'Espona, Andreu Arriola, Adolf Mon-clús Jurado, 1992), the ring road has now been demolished to create a ground level and underground road hub and a new urban public park.
The 34-storey elliptical tower for the headquarters of the company Aguas de Barcelona (AGBAR) is 142-metres high with a parabolic shaped roof and it's 350-seat auditorium. A striking feature is the façade's glass shutter system that lights up with changing colours at night, controlled by sophisticated Led technology. The architect, Jean Nouvel, was inspired by the towers of Gaudí's Sagrada Familia and the peaks of the Montserrat mountains. But the main idea was inspired by the commissioning client, the Barcelona Water Company. Nouvel described the design as "a fluid mass that bursts through the ground like a geyser under permanent, calculated pressure".

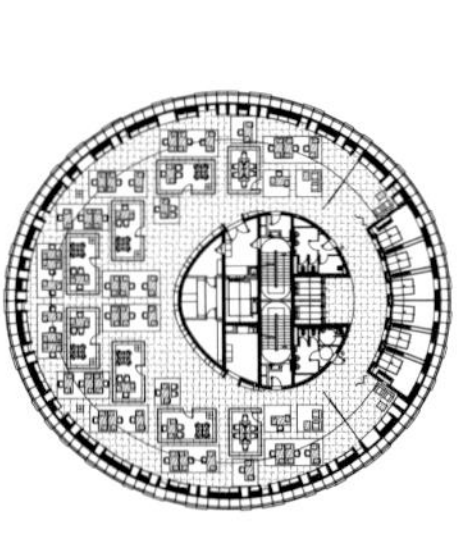

architects
Ateliers Jean Nouvel,
b720 Fermín Vázquez
Arquitectos (local architects)

type
office

construction
1999 - 2005

23. Diagonal 197

Avinguda Diagonal, 197
08018, Barcelona

external viewing only

L1 > Glòries

Stretching from the Torre Agbar, along the first section of the Avinguda Diagonal, a large number of new predominantly office buildings, form a multifaceted wall that is distinctly high-tech. In line with the sector 22@ plan, many industrial complexes were demolished or converted to house activities linked with new technologies. Among these, the Diagonal 197 building is the closest to Plaça de les Glòries and is visually connected with the tall shimmering tower designed by Jean Nouvel.
The Chipperfield building is an office skyscraper composed of two distinct sections: the lower, rhomboid-shaped block is 10 storeys high and is aligned with Avinguda Diagonal, while the taller 17 storey trapezoidal building, more slender and set back on the plot, is aligned at the rear with the Torre Agbar. The building clearly bears the mark of David Chipperfield for the modular composition of the cladding that adds rhythm to the façades. They are faced with a material that seems like natural stone, because of its earthy colours. The random pattern is composed of alternating prefabricated reinforced concrete panels in two sizes: 1.2×3 metres and 0.6×3 metres. Opaque windows with the same proportions are set between the coloured panels.

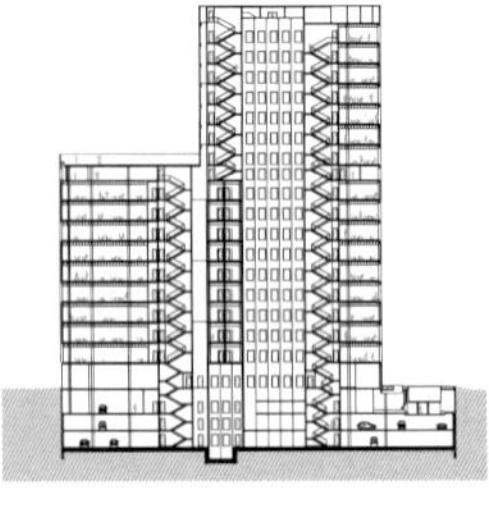

architects
David Chipperfield Architects,
b720 Fermín Vázquez Arquitectos

type
offices

construction
2008

24. MediaPro

Avinguda Diagonal, 177
08018, Barcelona

open to the public

L1 > Glòries

This building, designed by the architectural firm founded by Catalan architect, Carlos Ferrater, is the headquarters of a renowned audiovisual company. The structure is deliberately minimalist, composed of a bronze-painted steel and glass skin on a very complex framework that was adapted to the irregular shape of the plot. The main façade of the tower block containing the entrance to the building, is aligned with Avinguda Diagonal, creating a visual connection with the other office blocks that form the wall that begins in Plaça de les Glòries. The other street that influences the layout, is Carrer de Tànger, with which the lower block is aligned. It is set back from the Diagonal, in order to create a triangular open space.
An archway, created by removing the first 4 floors of the tower, where it dovetails into the base building, frames the urban landscape and generates an extra floor, aligned with Carrer Bolivia, which has the same side façades as the tower.

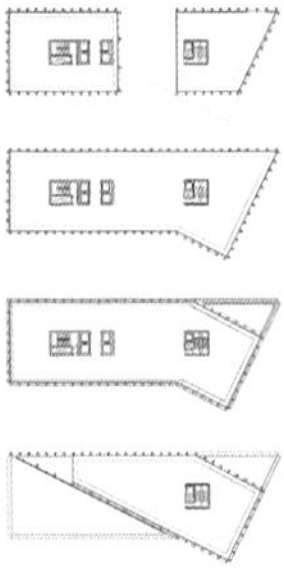

architects
OAB – Office of Architecture in Barcelona (Carlos Ferrater, Xavier Martí), Patrick Genard

type
multi-purpose complex

construction
2005 - 2008

25. Universitat Pompeu Fabra

Carrer de Tànger, 122
08018, Barcelona

open to the public

+34 93 542 20 00

www.upf.edu

L4 > Llacuna
L1 > Glòries

In line with the 22@ sector designation, the Poblenou section of the Universitat Pompeu Fabra (UPF) offers courses in digital creation, journalism, and communications, particularly focused on audiovisual media.

The university is built on the same site as the Can Framis Foundation, and based on the footprint of the former industrial plant, while aligning the structure with the Cerdá grid system. The complex is composed of two blocks of different size, shape and height. The first, along Carrer de Tànger, is four storeys high and clad in stone, while the second block set on pillars, has a plaster finish. An open space, planted with trees, has been created where the two buildings intersect, marking the entrance to the complex.

©Nomen arquitectes i associats

© Manuel Giron Perez

architects
Nomen arquitectes
i associats

type
university premises

construction
2009

26. Campus del Poblenou

Carrer de Roc Boronat, 138
08018, Barcelona

open to the public

+34 93 542 20 00

www.upf.edu/web/campus/campus-poblenou

L1 > Glòries

The Universitat Pompeu Fabra (UPF) campus is built on the same site as the Media-Pro building, opposite the university headquarters designed by Nomen arquitectes. The Campus occupies the site of the former Ca l'Aranyó textile factory, one of the oldest and most emblematic buildings in Barcelona's industrial history. The various sections of the factory were restored and converted, including the large central courtyard which has been transformed into the campus, featuring the factory's imposing chimney stack. The project includes a range of elements of the former industrial buildings, like the façades and structural framework composed of wrought iron pillars and girders, Catalan vaults and roof trusses. The new building façades contrast visually and tectonically with the old structures. The old pavilions and warehouses with their aged brick façades, have been integrated with the new constructions and materials. The contrast is harmonious and brings variety to the high tech surroundings in this part of Avinguda Diagonal.

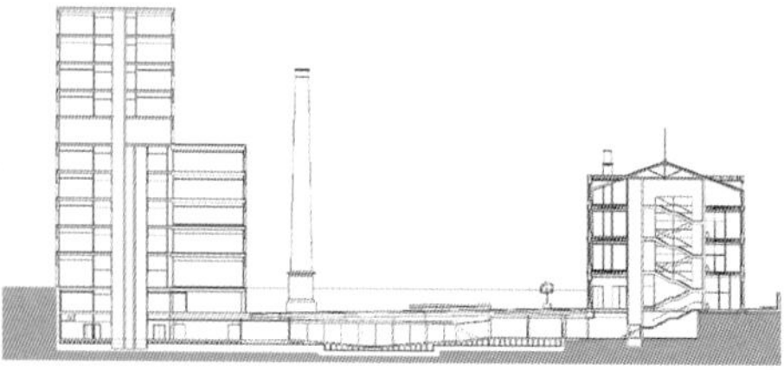

architects
Josep Benedito, Ramon Valls
(RQP Arquitectura)

type
campus

construction
2008 - 2016

27. Oficines Indra

Carrer de Roc Boronat, 133
08018, Barcelona

external viewing only

L1 > Glòries
L4 > Llacuna

The office block for the Indra technology company is built on a site following the demolition of former industrial buildings in a district now destined for new technologies, including the nearby MediaTIC building. The Indra building is composed of a prismatic 10-storey tower set on a 3-storey rhombic base, aligned with Carrer de Tànger, following the chamfered angle of the site. Between the tower and the base is a recessed technical services level, set back from the façade to enhance the floating effect and sense of lightness. The entire façade skin is made of stainless steel to provide internal protection from direct sunlight. Many of the mesh panels are stamped with a protruding or indented sphere recalling the company logo, as an means of immediate identification.

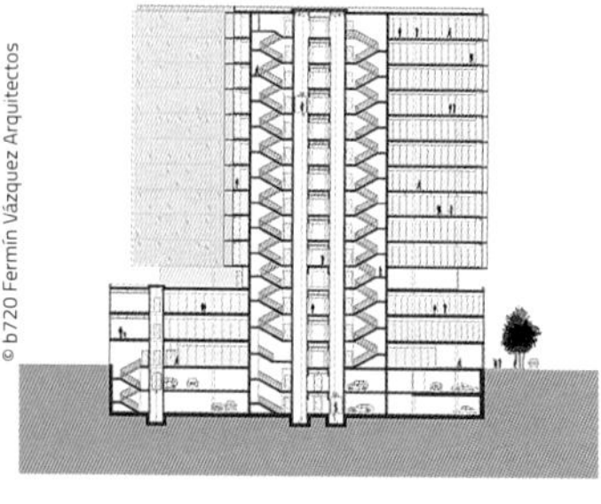

architects
b720 Fermín Vázquez Arquitectos

type
offices

construction
2006

28. MediaTIC

Carrer de Roc Boronat, 117
08018, Barcelona

Mon - Fri / 8 am - 8 pm
Sat - Sun / closed

+34 93 312 30 10

L1 > Glòries
L4 > Llacuna

The MediaTIC is an innovative structure promoted by the Consorci Zona Franca de Barcelona, and interprets the technological destination of Sector 22@ in an architectural key. It also incorporates its destination as a meeting point for companies and professionals on an even wider scale. Companies and institutions housed in the building include the BCN Activa, Thoughtworks, Softonic, Fundation Mobile World Capital, RMIT and Deloitte. The structure is based on a metal skeleton composed of four rigid braced frames that provide open modular space, abundant light and maximum flexibility. An internal courtyard crosses the whole building. The four façades, all different from one another, are clad in a special bright green polymer material (ETFE, Ethylene tetrafluoroethylene), that absorbs light captured during the day, providing insulation and considerable energy savings.

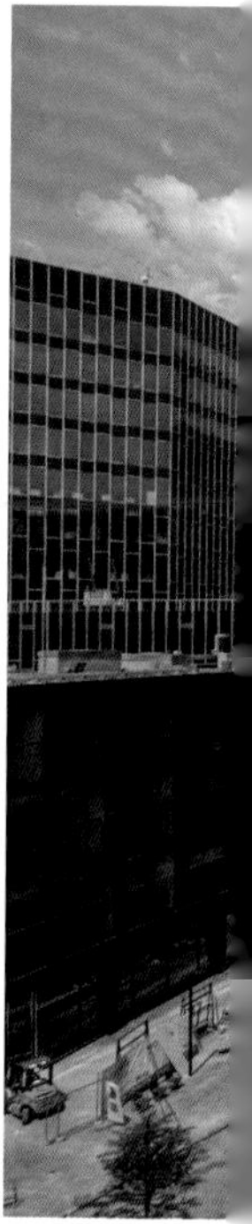

© Consorci Zona Franca Barcelona

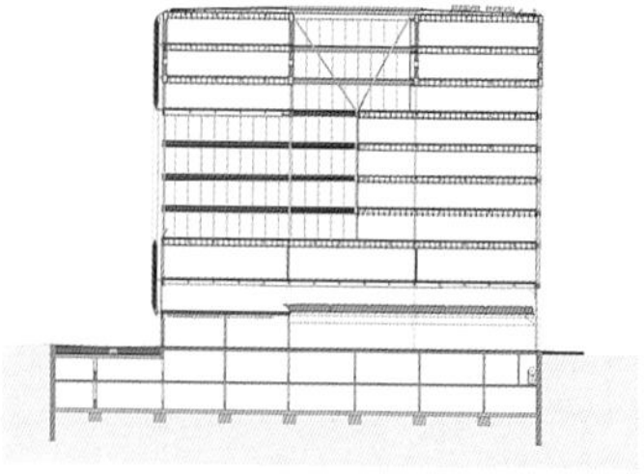

architects
Enric Ruiz-Geli

type
offices

construction
2009

29. Museu Can Framis

Carrer de Roc Boronat, 116-126
08018, Barcelona

Mon / closed
Tue - Sat / 11 am - 6 pm
Sun / 11 am - 2 pm

www.fundaciovilacasas.com

L4 > Llacuna

The museum is located in the 22@ district, currently undergoing widespread redevelopment to reconvert the former industrial area and its abandoned plants and factories into a new tertiary and technological hub. The project involves high density, vertical construction. Based on a concept of contrasts, this new exhibition space will become a calm, quiet art haven, surrounded by closely planted trees.
Two former industrial buildings (selected for their local historical role more than their architectural value) were preserved and renovated, then connected by a new transversal structure to form a courtyard that acts as an external entrance.
Visits begin on the top floor and follow a route descending through dimly lit spaces where all focus is concentrated on the artworks. Wooden elements highlight stairs, window and door openings, and the transition areas between the various structures.
A lime plaster finish harmonises the original façades blending with the exposed concrete of the new constructions: the façades form a "collage" of different textures that reflect the various layers and interventions the buildings have undergone over the years.

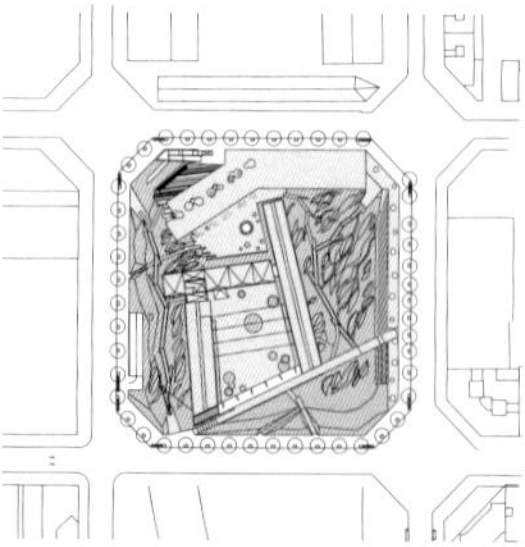

© BAAS Arquitectura

architects
BAAS Arquitectura

type
museum

construction
2009

30. Escola Sant Martí

Carrer de Sant Joan de Malta, 130
08018, Barcelona

external viewing only

+34 93 624 02 40
ceipsantmarti@xtec.cat
www.escolasantmartibcn.cat

L4 > Poblenou

This complex contains primary and secondary schools, an adult education centre, children's playcentre, plus two floors of undergound parking. The need to incorporate so many facilities in a limited space, restricted by urban regulations, inspired a design composed of parallel, solid and void horizontal bands for maximum light, natural ventilation and views of the internal spaces. The main school facilities are located on the ground floor, while all the first level roofing has been used to create playground areas. A large plinth base, set underground with the parking areas provides an impression of the whole school building as a huge perforated roof containing a range of open internal spaces (patios, courtyards, gardens, playing fields, urban vegetable plots). The building is arranged and coordinated in relation to these spaces.
The external impression of the school is sober and uniform, to blend with the surrounding neighbourhood. However, the interior is vibrant with bright colour. Special attention was paid to the constructive and technological solutions for the façades and roofing which has resulted in the building receiving Class A Energy Certification.

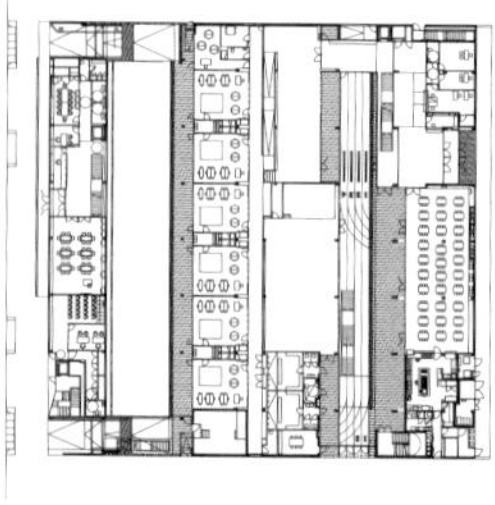

© SUMO Arquitectes

architects
SUMO Arquitectes,
Yolanda Olmo

type
school

construction
2013

31. Sala Beckett – Obrador Internacional de Dramatúrgia

Carrer de Pere IV, 228-232
08005, Barcelona

open to the public

+34 93 284 53 12
info@salabeckett.cat.
www.salabeckett.cat

L4 > Poblenou

This project involved the conversion of the former Cooperativa De Consumo Pau i Justícia di Poble Nou, a space where weddings, first communions, and other events were celebrated; although it had been abandoned for several years, it had remained strong in the memory of the local inhabitants. It was transformed to house a theatre and acting centre.
The project was studied carefully to respect the former structure, studying the original spaces and decoration in order to recover the same atmosphere in the new theatre centre.
A large atrium connects the various levels through wide openings that provide abundant light and views of the entire interior. Most of the rooms on the ground floor are used for public activities in order to maintain contact and continuity with the surrounding urban fabric.
The rehearsal rooms are on the first floor, together with another space, an ex-ballroom, which can be used for workshops or as a second theatre. The second floor houses more rehearsal rooms and service spaces.

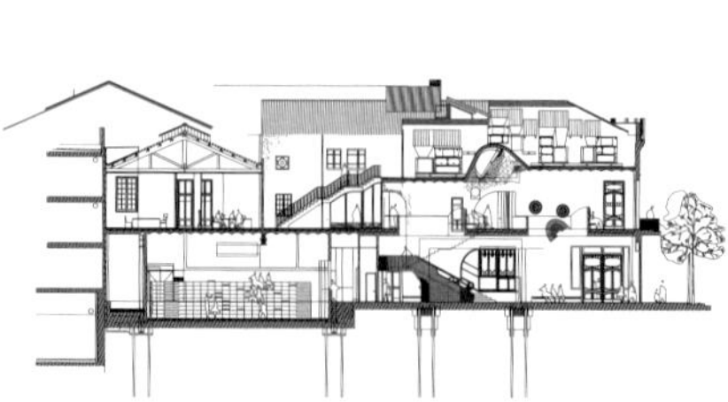

© Flores & Prats

architects
Flores & Prats

type
multi-purpose complex

construction
2016

32. Meliá Barcelona Sky

Carrer de Pere IV, 272
08005, Barcelona

open to the public

+34 93 367 20 50
melia.sky@melia.com
www.melia.com

L4 > Poblenou

Together with the Hines 123 building, immediately adjacent and also designed by Dominique Perrault, the Meliá Barcelona Sky tower is an iconic piece of architecture that makes a strong impact on the urban landscape as it is visible for miles. The Hotel is composed of a soaring tower, 120 metres high, a rectangular parallelepiped split lengthwise in two, with one half "slid" skywards, seeming to defy gravity. At the base of the tower, a lower block houses the hotel foyer, restaurants, meeting rooms, swimming pool, café and bar, while the tower contains the 259 rooms, all facing the sea or the mountains and with views of the Sagrada Familia. The façade is clad in panels of anodised aluminium, alternating with the window openings. The overall effect is extremely ethereal, like a steel shard thrust into the ground alongside the Diagonal.

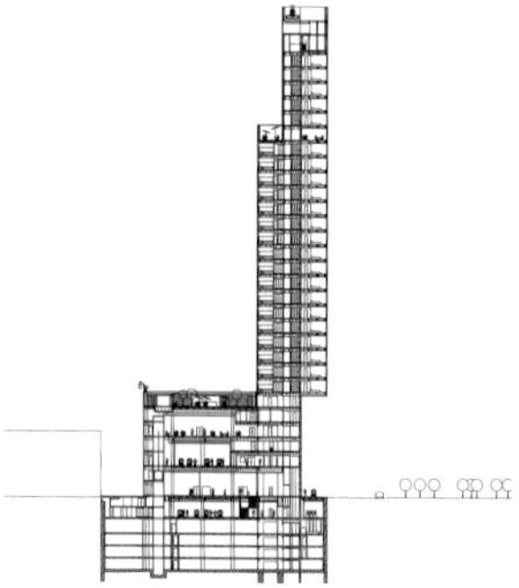

architects
Dominique Perrault
Architecture

type
hotel

construction
1999 - 2008

33. Oficines Hines 123

Avinguda Diagonal, 123
08005, Barcelona

external viewing only

L4 > Poblenou

This building, and the adjacent hotel Meliá Barcelona Sky, also designed by Dominique Perrault, marks the entrance to the seafront districts and is a landmark for those travelling along the Avinguda Diagonal. The rectangular building, aligned with the Diagonal, is split in half; the top portion is displaced forwards, projecting out towards the Carrer de Lope de Vega. The space created on the other side forms a terrace facing the street with sea views. A building in motion, rather like a sculpture in black glass with fine lines of gleaming silver. At night the glass lights up and becomes transparent.

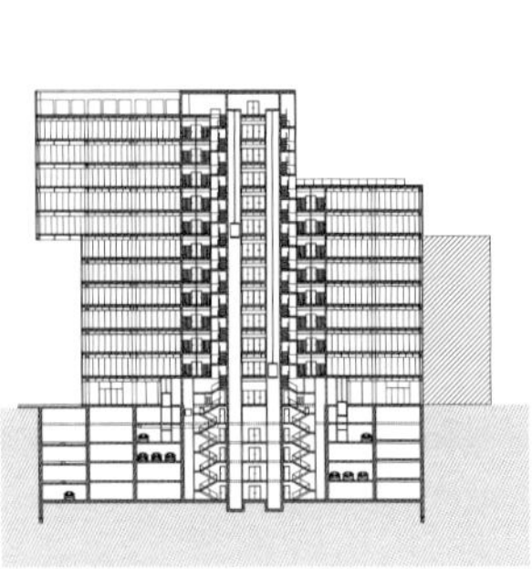

architects
Dominique Perrault Architecture

type
offices

construction
2003 - 2009

34. Mental Disabled Residence and Day Centre

Gran Via, 970
08018, Barcelona

open to the public

L2 > Bac de Roda

This building is "inserted" between two tall apartment blocks 9-10 storeys high, but the height of this building was limited to 3 storeys. The architects managed to transform the restrictions imposed by functional requirements and the limited site with a design on different levels, arranged around an internal courtyard garden to reproduce the feelings of living in a villa. The Gran Via façade is a translucent wall with a lattice surface, much lower than the adjacent buildings, and crowned by a garden. Protected from the outward, the building looks to its center: the courtyard that divides the building lengthwise into two sections. The cross-section shows how the residential spaces, and above all, the circulation and common areas, are built around a green planted courtyard so that all spaces receive natural light and views of nature. The principle uses of this building – the day centre and residence, are divided according to various levels rather than size, in order to reduce vertical circulation to a minimum. The residence is located on the first and second floors while the day centre, shared by residents and foreign users is placed on the ground floor and mezzanine.

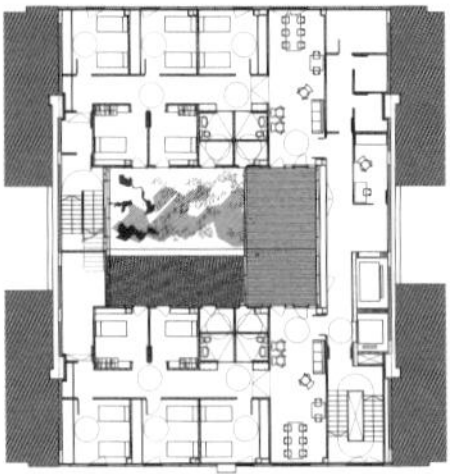

architects
aldayjover arquitectura
y paisaje

type
healthcare centre

construction
2008

35. Parc Diagonal Mar

Carrer de Llull, 350
08019, Barcelona

Mon - Sun / 10 am - 10 pm

L4 > Selva de Mar

In the 1990s, as part of the project to transform the Diagonal Mar industrial area, in addition to constructing a residential quarter with high-rise buildings, it was also decided to create a vast park, whose design was assigned to the Miralles-Tagliabue firm. The park area is bordered by the Avinguda Diagonal, and the Ronda Litoral, a high-speed highway parallel to the coastline, and also surrounded by tower blocks. The large green space is divided by a "tree" system of routes that branch out in different directions. The main avenue connects the Avinguda Diagonal directly with the waterfront, and includes a pedestrian bridge that crosses the Ronda Litoral. The walk paths are packed earth paved with multicoloured tiles, or routes through green spaces which incorporate play areas, skating and biking paths. The park has several water features: ponds, fountains and above all, a large lake located alongside the entire length of the main avenue. Next to the lake, there are spacious seating areas with pergola structures made from curved metal piping; some support ceramic plant pots decorated with trencadís mosaics recalling those by Gaudí, but these are an element that has always been dear to Miralles. The park represents a green oasis in an area with problems that are not yet resolved. The intensive residential program has not managed to become integrated in the urban fabric, nor has it been able to impose its own personal identity.

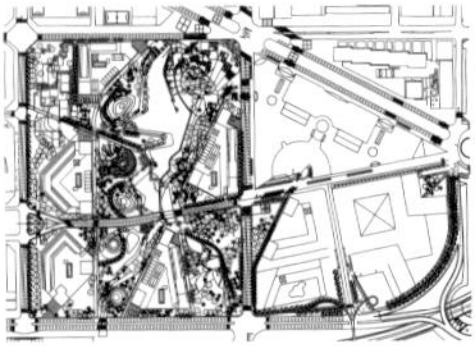

© Miralles Tagliabue EMBT

architects
Miralles Tagliabue EMBT

type
park

construction
2002

36. CCIB Centre de Convencions Internacionals de Barcelona

Plaça de Willy Brandt, 11-14
08019, Barcelona

open to the public

+34 93 230 10 00

www.ccib.es

L4 > El Maresme | Fòrum

The CCIB International Convention Centre was built as part of the 2004 Forum of Cultures, a large event that definitively marked the transformation of the eastern part of the city. The building sits in the so-called Plaça del Fòrum, a 40 acre platform in multicoloured concrete on the seafront, designed by José Antonio Martínez Lapeña and Elías Torres. Passing over the new Ronda Litoral highway, the platform terminates with elongated quays that extend into the sea like long fingers. On one of these quays rises a vast 4 thousand square metre solar panel pergola, (José Antonio Martínez Lapeña, Elías Torres) and a pedestrian walkway (Mamen Domingo and Ernest Ferré) that bridges the water and leads to the Parc Litoral Nord (Iñaki Ábalos, Juan Herreros).
The CCIB, is composed of a group of buildings with a range of different functions. The congress centre has a very large 15,000 square metre hall, 80 metres high, that can be divided up according to necessity: it resembles a covered square open onto the seafront. The façade is clad in undulated metal panels that create an organic effect. On Carrer Taulat is the AC hotel with office spaces on the top floors.

© Mateo Arquitectura

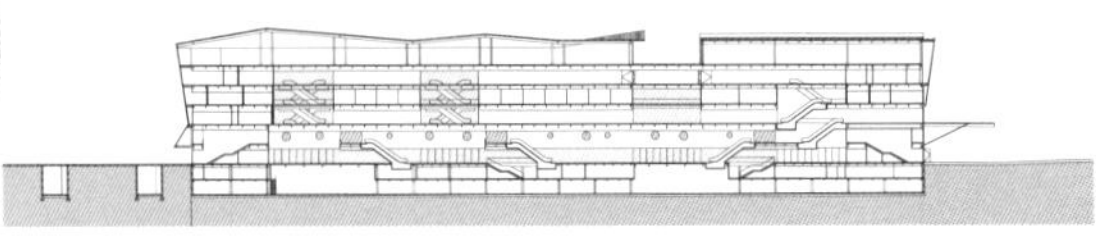

architects
Mateo Arquitectura

type
multi-purpose complex

construction
2004

37. Museu de Ciències Naturals de Barcelona

Plaça Leonardo da Vinci, 4-6
08019, Barcelona

October - February
Mon / closed
Tue - Fri / 10 am - 6 pm
Sat / 10 am - 7 pm
Sun / 10 am - 8 pm
March - September
Mon / closed
Tue - Sat / 10 am - 7 pm
Sun and holiday / 10 am - 8 pm

+34 93 256 60 02
museuciencies@bcn.cat
museuciencies.cat

L4 > El Maresme | Fòrum

Near the Diagonal Mar is the Museu de Ciències Naturals de Barcelona designed by Herzog & de Meuron: also known as the Fòrum Building, it is a cobalt blue, triangular structure that seems to float over the multicoloured platform constructed for the Forum of Cultures in 2004.
The building was designed to host a series of conferences and large-scale meetings, and included conference halls, exhibition spaces, and a vast auditorium. Even the site on which it was built was equipped to be used as a public space for open-air events. A series of openings were created in the structure to provide cones of light for the external spaces. Transferring the Natural Science Museum to the building involved redesigning the architecture since the building did not have a specific use following the Forum. The public space under the triangular body of the building has been modified, creating a vibrant external area for students and groups.

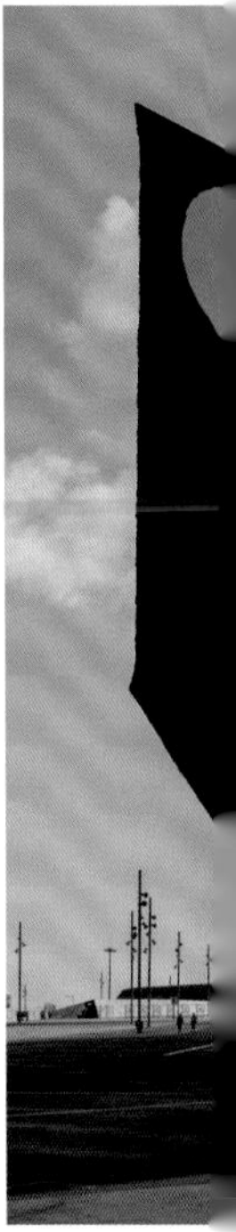

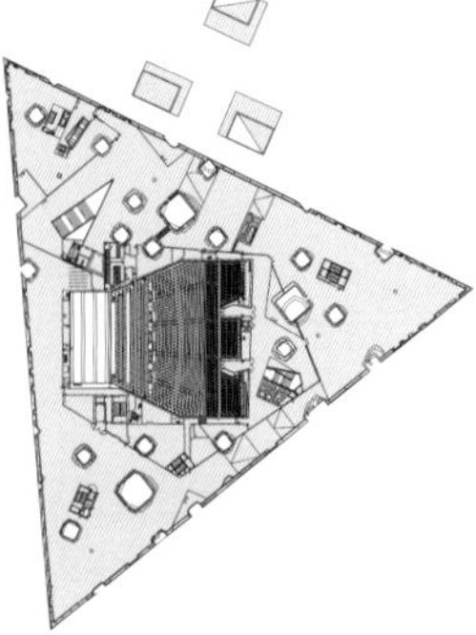

© Herzog & de Meuron

© JM deLlobet

architects
Herzog & de Meuron

type
museum

construction
2002-2004

38. Diagonal ZeroZero

Plaça d'Ernest
Lluch i Martin, 5
08019, Barcelona

external viewing only

L4 > El Maresme | Fòrum

Positioned next to the Fòrum area, the Gruppo Telefónica office building is a triangular trapezoidal prism, 110 metres high, made of glass and white steel.
The tower rises at the beginning of the Avinguda Diagonal marking the access to the sea. A powerful example of high-tech architecture, the core is built of concrete with an external structure in steel, divided into two sections: an internal vertical structure composed of slender H pillars, and an external bracing lattice that can withstand flection stress and torque. The lattice is composed of white aluminium profiles and extra-clear glass with white ceramic paint serigraphy.

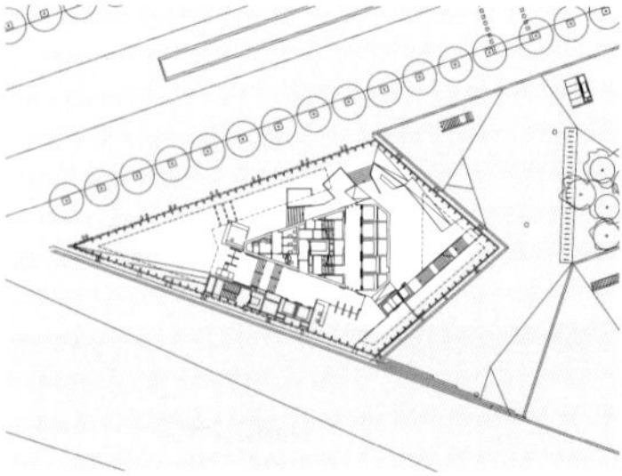

© EMBA

architects
EMBA – Estudi Massip-Bosch Architects

type
corporate headquarters

construction
2006 - 2011

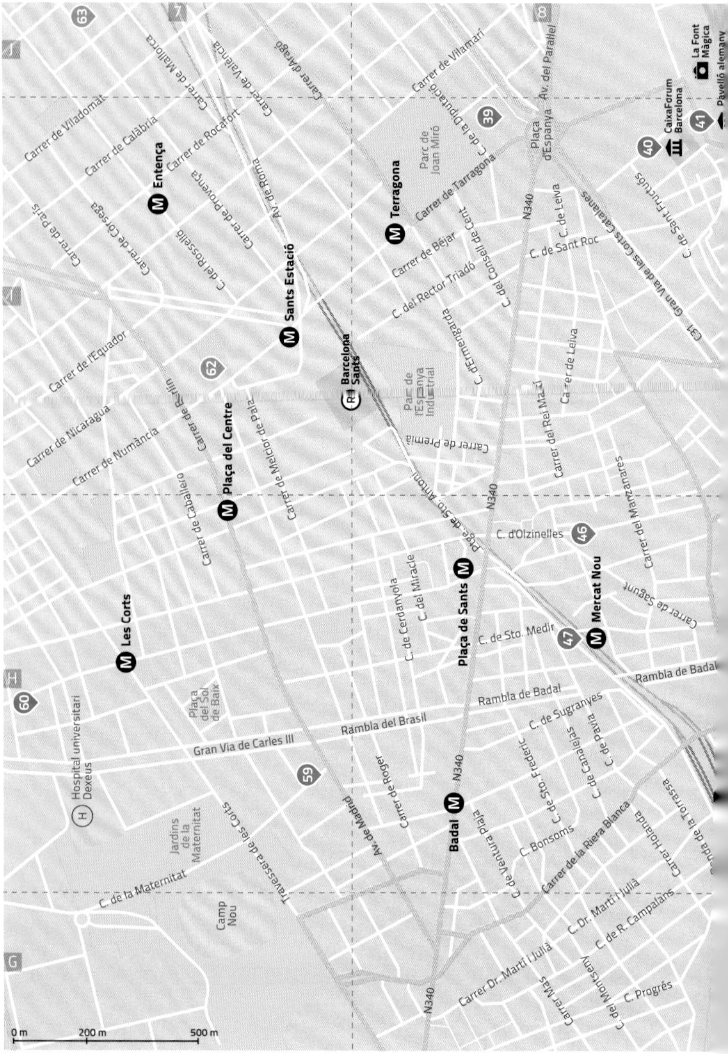
Carrer de Viladomat
Carrer de Calàbria
Carrer de Mallorca
Carrer de Rocafort
Carrer de València
Carrer d'Aragó
Entença
Carrer de París
Carrer de Còrsega
C. del Rosselló
Carrer de Provença
Av. de Roma
Sants Estació
Carrer de Vilamarí
C. de la Diputació
Parc de Joan Miró
Carrer de Tarragona
Terragona
Plaça d'Espanya
Av. del Paral·lel
CaixaForum Barcelona
La Font Màgica
Pavelló alemany
Carrer de l'Equador
Carrer de Nicaragua
Carrer de Numància
Carrer de Caballero
Plaça del Centre
Carrer de Melcior de Palau
Barcelona Sants
Parc de l'Espanya Industrial
Carrer de Premià
Carrer de Béjar
C. del Rector Triadó
C. del Consell de Cent
C. d'Ermengarda
N340
C. de Leiva
C. de Sant Roc
Gran Via de les Corts Catalanes
C. de Sant Fructuós
C31
Carrer de Leiva
Carrer del Rei Martí
Carrer del Manzanares
C. d'Olzinelles
Mercat Nou
Carrer de Sagunt
Les Corts
Plaça de Sants
C. del Miracle
C. de Cerdanyola
C. de Sto. Medir
Rambla de Badal
Hospital universitari Dexeus
Plaça del Sol de Baix
Gran Via de Carles III
Rambla del Brasil
C. de Sugranyes
C. de Sto. Frederic
C. de Canalejas
C. de Pavia
Carrer de Roger
Av. de Madrid
Badal
Travessera de les Corts
Jardins de la Maternitat
C. de la Maternitat
Camp Nou
C. de Ventura Plaja
C. Bonsoms
Carrer de la Riera Blanca
Carrer Holanda
C. Dr. Martí i Julià
Carrer Dr. Martí i Julià
C. de R. Campalans
Carrer Mas
C. del Montseny
C. Progrés
Ronda de la Torrassa
0 m
200 m
500 m
63
60
62
59
39
40
41
46
47
7
8
J
I
H
G

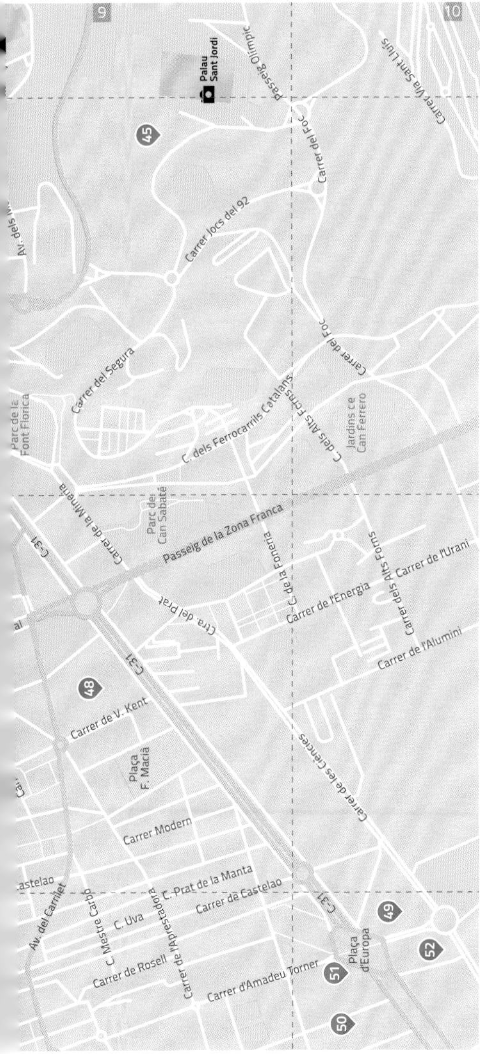

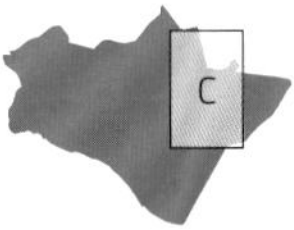

Montjuïc – Llobregat

39. Las Arenas de Barcelona
40. CaixaForum Barcelona
41. Pavelló alemany – Pavelló Mies van der Rohe – Pavelló Barcelona
42. Museu Nacional d'Art de Catalunya
43. Fundació Joan Miró
44. Jardí Botànic de Barcelona
45. Torre de telecomunicaciones de Montjuïc – Calatrava Tower
46. La Lleialtat Santsenca
47. Jardins de la Rambla de Sants
48. Ciutat de la Justicia
49. Edificio Plaça d'Europa 31
50. Puig Tower
51. Barcelona Metro Line 9
52. Hotel Porta Fira
53. Parc Logístic de la Zona Franca
54. Power plant of Barcelona South / Zona Franca
55. Parc Esportiu Llobregat
56. Oficina Registre Civil
57. Taller de Arquitectura La Fàbrica
58. Nexus II
59. Centre Cívic Joan Oliver "Pere Quart"
60. Roca Barcelona Gallery

39. Las Arenas de Barcelona

Gran Via Corts Catalanes, 373-385
08015, Barcelona

June - September
Mon - Sat / 10 am - 10 pm
Sun / closed
October - May
Mon - Sat / 9 am - 9 pm
Sun / closed

+34 93 289 02 44
arenas.informacion@arenasdebarcelona.com
www.arenasdebarcelona.com

L3 > Tarragona

Rogers Stirk Harbour and Partners' design, with co-architect Alonso y Balaguer, for completely restoring the historical Plaça de Toros – out of use since 1977 – involved removing every element inside the original shell structure. It represents a true example of the architects' technical vision which uses structural expression and architectural flexibility as the main bases for their design: "long life, loose fit, low energy". The only remaining element of the original bull ring – even though it is cut at street level to provide full access at this level – is the circular brick façade decorated in neomudéjar style, typical of bull ring architecture. The outer wall has become a separate enclosure, with support systems attached to new independent internal pylon structures. The layout maintains its original circular form. The steel structural and connecting elements are vibrantly coloured and recall tradition and imagery of the bullring and the revolutionary high-tech aesthetics of the Pompidou Centre designed by Piano + Rogers in 1977. An office and retail building is placed down one side of Las Arenas to create a street frontage to Calle Llança.

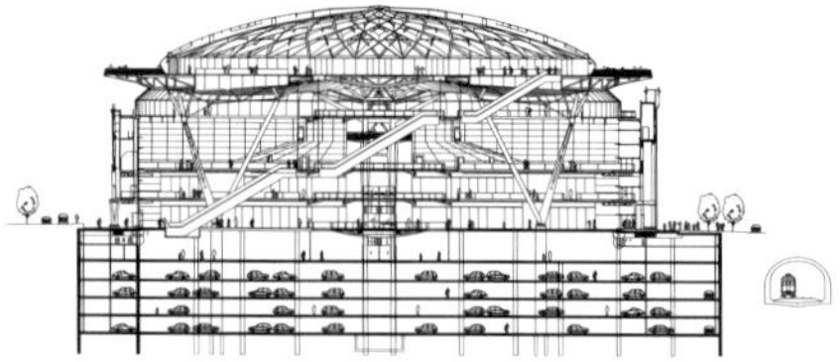

architects
Rogers Stirk Harbour + Partners, Alonso y Balaguer

type
exhibition centre, retail

construction
2011

40. CaixaForum Barcelona

Avinguda de Francesc Ferrer i Guàrdia, 6-8
08038, Barcelona

Mon - Sun / 10 am - 8 pm

+34 93 476 86 00

caixaforum.es

L1 > Hostafrancs

In 1911, the Catalan architect, Josep Puig i Cadafalch, designed a majestic textile factory that today houses the CaixaForum Barcelona.
The Fàbrica Casaramona is a modernist building of great architectural merit, and was declared as a monument of national interest in 1976. Left empty for many years, in 1993, it was purchased by the Fundació "la Caixa", one of the most important Spanish banks, and later converted into a multifunctional cultural centre. The restoration work (1999-2002) preserved the original open spatial concept, and added a projecting entrance on the secondary façade, designed by the Japanese architect, Arata Isozaki. A large sculptural shelter in the form of two stylised trees, in cor-ten steel and glass, gives access to a sunken courtyard that runs the length of the original building, and a series of parallel walls guide visitors towards the hall in the basement. The basement space is entirely faced in white limestone. The new space does not cover the original building but creates a contrast to the shape and colour of the exposed red brick.

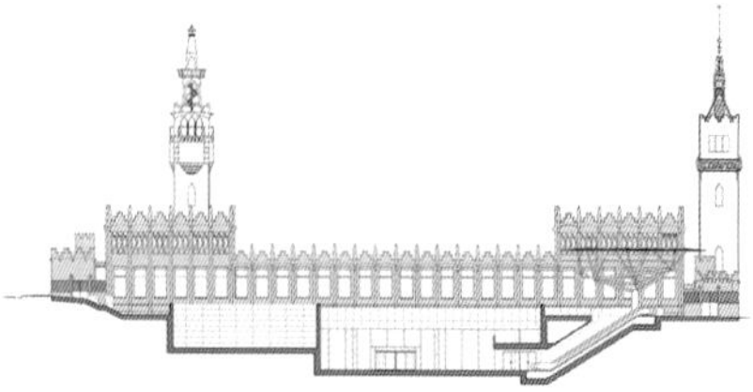

architects
Arata Isozaki
(new entrance)

type
cultural centre

construction
2002 (restoration
+ new entrance)

41. Pavelló alemany – Pavelló Mies van der Rohe – Pavelló Barcelona

Avinguda de Francesc Ferrer i Guàrdia, 7
08038, Barcelona

March - October
Mon - Sun / 10 am - 8 pm
November - February
Mon - Sun / 10 am - 6 pm

+34 93 215 10 11
pavellomies@miesbcn.com
miesbcn.com

L1 > Espanya

In 1929, Germany commissioned the modernist architect, Ludwig Mies van der Rohe to design a pavilion to host the German authorities during the International Exposition in Barcelona. The pavilion is considered the peak of the architect's early career. Together with the Tugendhat house (1930) and the model home for the *Construction Exhibition* in Berlin (1931), it is the emblematic composition of the "Free Plan" concept. The lengthwise layout of the space is defined with the use of independent orthogonal walls highlighted by the combination of different surface materials. Set on an opaque travertine plinth, a long wall runs the length of an outdoor space containing a large reflecting pool. The interior layout is defined by a wall in polished onyx and terminates in an enclosed courtyard. The flat slab roof is supported by eight cruciform steel columns. As an additional feature for the pavilion, Mies van der Rohe and Lilly Reich designed a chromed steel and leather chair, which has become an icon of modern design.
The pavilion was dismantled at the end of the event, but in 1986 it was faithfully reconstructed to its original design, and in the same location. The sculpture in the background is also an identical reproduction of the original by George Kolbe, which disappeared in 1930.

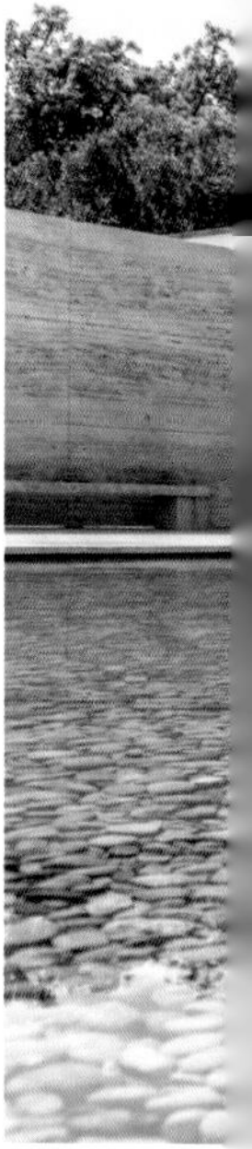

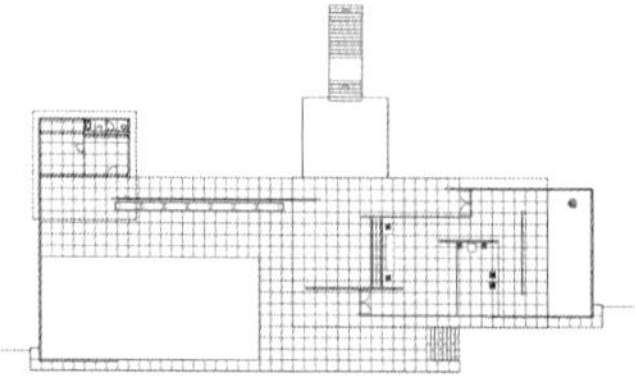

architects
Ludwing Mies van der Rohe /
Ignasi de Solà-Morales,
Cristian Cirici, Fernando
Ramos (reconstruction)

type
museum

construction
1929 /
1986 (reconstruction)

42. Museu Nacional d'Art de Catalunya

Palau Nacional,
Parc de Montjuïc
08038, Barcelona

October - April
Mon / closed
Tue - Sat / 10 am - 6 pm
2 May - 30 September
Mon / closed
Tue - Sat / 10 am - 8 pm

Sun and Holidays /
10 am - 3 pm

www.museunacional.cat

L3 > Poble Sec

The Montjuïc hill rises over the south-western side of the city offering a wide range of activities. For the Universal Exposition in 1929, the hill was chosen as the site for the construction of magnificent public buildings including the Palau Nacional – today home to the Museu Nacional d'Art de Catalunya – and was later subject to radical urban transformation for the 1992 Olympic Games. The imposing Neo-Baroque architecture of the Palau Nacional can be seen on the Montjuïc hillside from all panoramic points in the city. Converted to a museum in 1934, it hosts a vast collection of Catalan art ranging from the Dark Ages to the early 20th century, and is one of the major symbols of Catalan Separatist identity (in contrast with the original nationalist role established under the dictatorship of Miguel Primo de Rivera). During the 1990s, it was restored and renovated with a striking staging design by the Italian architect, Gae Aulenti.

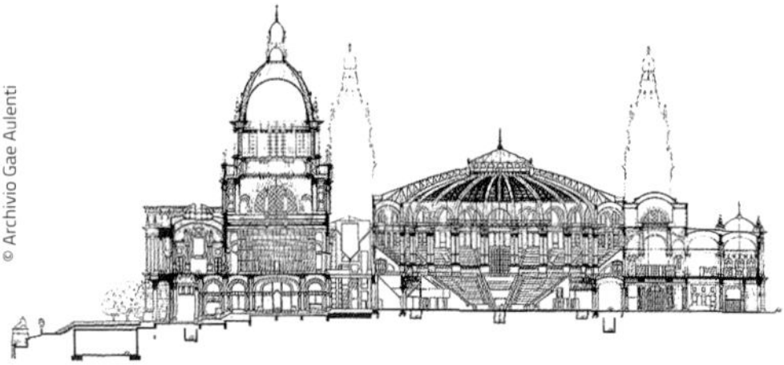

© Museu Nacional d'Art de Catalunya

architects
Eugenio Pedro Cendoya, Enric Catà, Pere Domènech i Roura / Gae Aulenti (extension and restoration)

type
museum

construction
1929 / 1997 (extension and restoration)

43. Fundació Joan Miró

Parc de Montjuïc
08038, Barcelona

November - March
Tue, Wed, Fri / 10 am - 6 pm
April - October
Tue, Wed, Fri / 10 am - 8 pm
Thu / 10 am - 9 pm
Sat / 10 am - 8 pm
Sun / 10 am - 3 pm
Mon / closed

+34 93 443 94 70
info@fmirobcn.org
www.fmirobcn.org

Montjuïc Funicular >
Paral·lel - Parc de Montjuïc (metro Paral·lel, integrated fare)

55 / 150 >
Parc de Montjuïc

In 1975, two great Catalan figures collaborated to create one of the most innovative experimental museums on the international scene. Joan Miró, one of the most influential artists of the 20th century, decided to set up a foundation to permit access to and the diffusion of not only his own work, but contemporary art in general. Set in the Montjuïc Hill, the building was designed by the architect Josep Lluís Sert, based on the principles of rationalist architecture, blended with elements of traditional Mediterranean vernacular. The white concrete and glass complex features a dynamic layout with exhibition rooms arranged around a central courtyard, and magnificent views over the city and the gardens that surround the building. It is the result of perfect correlation between Miró's artistic expression and Sert's architectural language; the two men were very close friends and had previously worked together. The foundation has been extended in 1988 and 2000 by Jaume Freixa, Sert's friend and pupil.

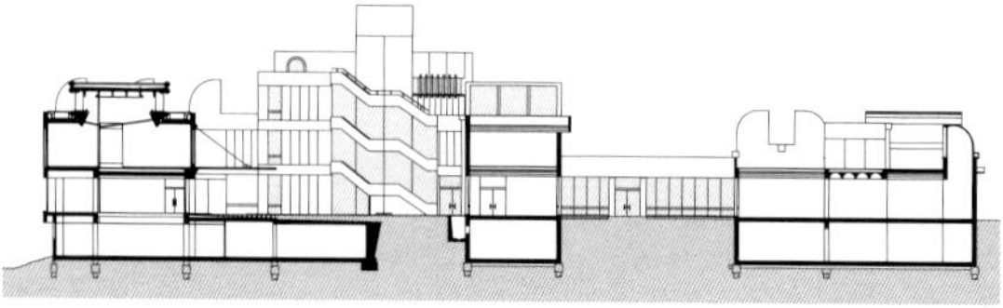

architects
Josep Lluís Sert / Jaume Freixa
(extension and restoration)

type
museum

construction
1972 / 1987 - 2001
(extension and restoration)

44. Jardí Botànic de Barcelona

Carrer Doctor i Font Quer
08038, Barcelona

January - March,
November - December
Mon - Sun / 10 am - 6 pm
April - May,
September - October
Mon - Sun / 10 am - 7 pm
June - August
Mon - Sun / 10 am - 8 pm

+34 93 256 41 60

L9 S > Fira

The Jardí Botànic is the combined project of a multidisciplinary and international team composed of two architects, a landscape architect, a horticulturist, and a biologist. The objective of this project, that transformed over 34 acres of landfill terrain, was aimed at having the least possible impact on the landscape, respecting the natural features as far as possible. The orography of Montjuïc Hill was the main inspiration for the project design that was centred around walking paths, water pools, and planted areas that were adapted to the natural altitude. The resulting layout is composed of 71 triangular areas that differ according to criteria that groups typical vegetation from five Mediterranean-type climatic regions throughout the world. The park is equipped with zero impact solar panel powered lighting and irrigation systems. All materials for the walkways and seating are recycled and environmentally friendly.

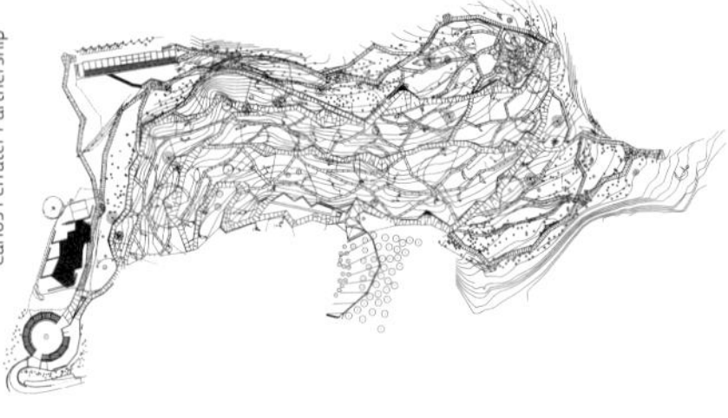

© Office of Architecture in Barcelona
Carlos Ferrater Partnership

architects
Carlos Ferrater, Jose Luis Canosa, Bet Figueras

type
park

construction
1999

45. Torre de telecomunicaciones de Montjuïc – Calatrava Tower

Carrer Pierre de Coubertin
08038, Barcelona

external viewing only

www.telefericdemontjuic.cat/es/torre-de-calatrava

L9 S > Fira

The "Olympic Ring of Montjuïc" is an urban park designed for the Barcelona Olympic Games in 1992 by Federico Correa and Alfons Milà. The park had formerly been used for the Universal Exposition in 1929, and was then abandoned. It is composed of a series of terraces that follow the slope of the Montjuïc Hill. The sports facilities, arranged along the sides of the axial route, were designed by various international architects including the Palau Sant Jordi by Arata Isozaki, and the INEFC headquarters by the team of Ricardo Bofill. Beginning with the Olympic Stadium, restored and extended at the same time, the route leads to a circular public square featuring the Montjuïc Communications Tower, 136 metres high. Designed by Santiago Calatrava, the sculptural form of the tower recalls the body of an athlete carrying the Olympic torch. The tower is built in steel and flexible concrete, and the base is decorated with mosaics that echo the trencadís technique used by Gaudí.

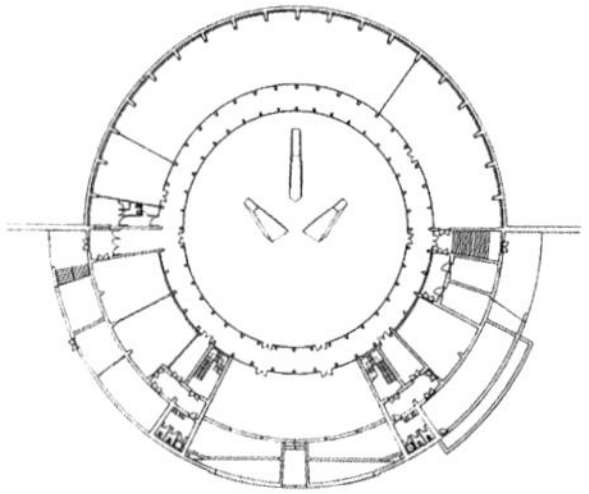

architects
Santiago Calatrava

type
infrastructure

construction
1989 - 1992

46. La Lleialtat Santsenca

Carrer d'Olzinelles, 31
08014, Barcelona

open to the public

+34 93 706 52 54
info@lleialtat.cat
www.lleialtat.cat

L1 > Mercat Nou

On the completion of a project involving the participation of the cultural associations of the Sants neighbourhood, in 2017, the celebrated "Lleialtat Santsenca" workers cooperative re-opened its headquarters, completely redesigned by the Harquitectes architectural firm. The restoration project upgraded the spaces and technology of the former 20th century building to modern standards, and despite having to demolish the damaged areas, they were able to maintain the historical value intact. In this way, the intense material stratification of the building was preserved, emphasising the architectural traces of the past. The three existing buildings were connected by a new metal structure supporting a double roof, using cellular polycarbonate for the side facing south, and sheet metal facing north. The lengthwise core of the building was left free for stairs and walkways to facilitate internal communication. The metal structure recalls work site scaffolding. The structure is designed as a bio-conditioned space with the use of specific building solutions to passively control the internal micro climate.

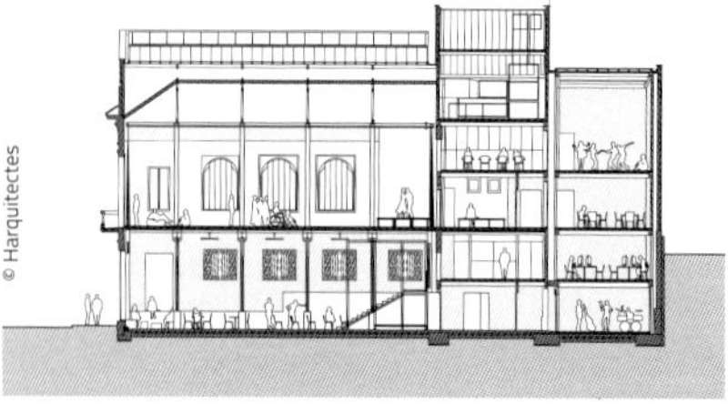

© Harquitectes

architects
Harquitectes

type
multi-purpose complex

construction
2016

47. Jardins de la Rambla de Sants

Carrer d'Antoni de Capmany
08014, Barcelona

open to the public

+34 93 402 70 00

L1 > Mercat Nou

The Jardins de la Rambla de Sants is an urban park covering over 31,300 square metres. It is designed as an elevated promenade built on a continuous raised structure constructed as a shell over the existing subway railway line. It was built in 2012 to abate the noise pollution that disturbed the surrounding area. The walkway is 760 metres long with an average width of 30 metres, at a height of between 6 and 14 metres above street level. Over 160 trees have been planted, as well as 85,000 native plants and shrubs, arranged in different areas. The project was based on strict criteria of environmental sustainability with Led lighting, solar panel energy and the re-use of rainwater. Ramps and elevators have been installed at 10 points along the route for access to the subway and streets below. At the end of the promenade, towards Hospitalet de Llobregat, is a complex with public rest rooms, restaurants, an educational garden, a children's play zone, a fitness area, and a thematic library.

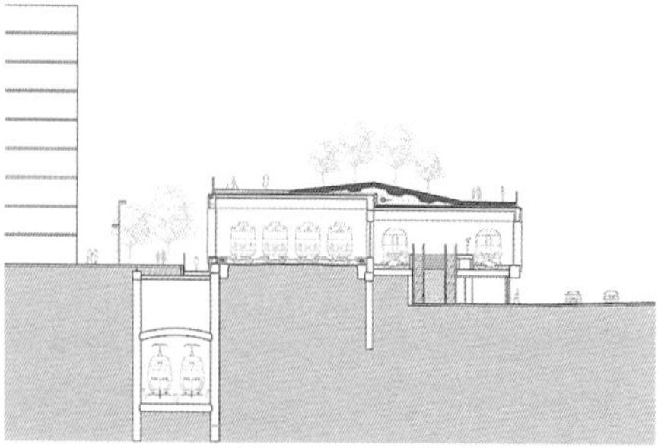

© Sergi Godia

architects
Sergi Godia, Ana Molino

type
park

construction
2016

48. Ciutat de la Justicia

Gran Via de les Corts Catalanes, 111
08014, Barcelona

Mon - Fri / 9 am - 2 pm
Sat - Sun / closed

+34 93 554 86 00

www.ciutatdelajusticia.com

L1 > Santa Eulàlia

This project, designed by David Chipperfield Architects, groups all the legal departments of the city in nine buildings located in a single urban area, strategically positioned on the border between Barcelona and Hospitalet de Llobregat, which is also adjacent to the access routes into the centre from the south. The project was based on dividing the various departments among different buildings, seven of which are arranged around a public square, while a short distance away are another two separate blocks, but connected by a low building that houses the courtrooms. All nine buildings are composed of compact blocks with coloured concrete façades. The buildings are accentuated by narrow rectangular windows that cover all the façades in a regular grid pattern. The various colours of all the tower blocks are in contrast with the base in sharp black and white.

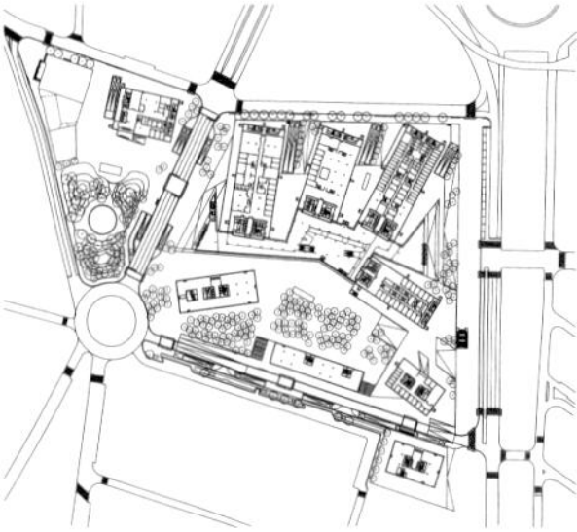

© David Chipperfield Architects

architects
David Chipperfield Architects,
b720 Fermín Vázquez
Arquitectos

type
multi-purpose complex

construction
2002 - 2011

49. Edificio Plaça d'Europa 31

L'Hospitalet de Llobregat
08908, Barcelona

external viewing only

L9 S > Fira

Plaça d'Europa is part of the urban strip between the "El Prat" airport and the centre of Barcelona which has undergone an almost complete urbanisation program in recent years forming an important commercial hub for the entire metropolitan area. The masterplan was designed by Albert Viaplana and is composed of a strict configuration of linear buildings and towers in a concentric curved layout around a central intersection. The style prescribed for the four buildings imposed a regulated three-part set-back stepped structure. One of the buildings was designed in 2011 by the Catalan firm, RCR Arquitectes – winner of the Pritzker Prize in 2017. This black compact building has an outer bearing structure composed of steel slatted ribs, set at different angles along the main façade.

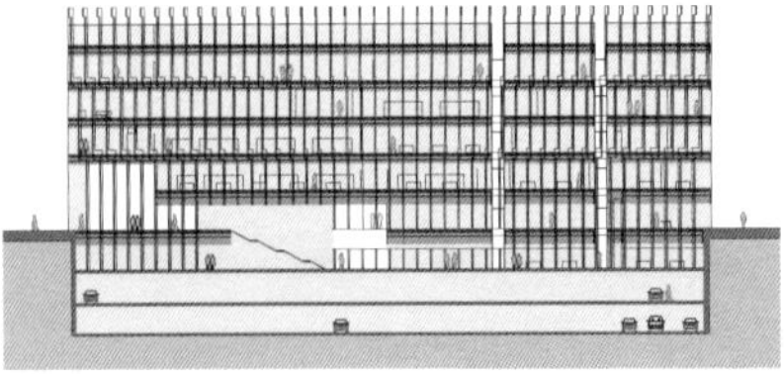

© RCR Arquitectes

architects
RCR Arquitectes

type
offices

construction
2008 - 2011

50. Puig Tower

Plaça d'Europa, 46-48,
L'Hospitalet de Llobregat
08902, Barcelona

open to the public

+34 93 400 70 00

www.puig.com

L9 S > Can Tries | Gornal

The plan by Albert Viaplana established a square floor plan with variable heights for the twelve tower buildings in the complex. Built between 2010 and 2015, the towers were designed by international architects and commissioned by private companies and destined for different functions and purposes. At the western end of the square, the Spanish multinational company, Puig, commissioned a new headquarters to celebrate the centenary of the company's foundation. It was designed by Rafael Moneo, the first Spaniard to have won the Pritzker Prize in 1996. The tower is 107 metres high and is based on a steel structure with continuous glazed façades. The internal space is modular and extremely flexible, arranged around a central core containing the stairs, elevator systems, and technical services. A fine ribbon-like element forms a unique spiral effect on the entire glass façade giving it great impact.

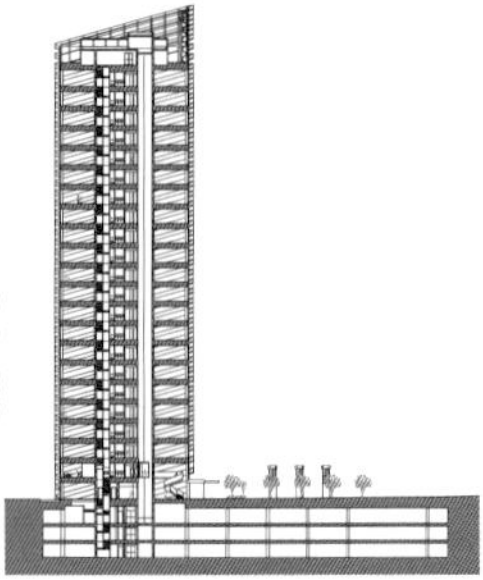

© Rafael Moneo

architects
Rafael Moneo, GCA Architects, Lucho Marcial

type
commercial hub, hotel, offices

construction
2015

51. Barcelona Metro Line 9

Aeroport T1 -
Zona Universitaria
Barcelona

open to the public

The project design for the three Metro stations, Europa-Fira, Parc Logístic and Mercabarna on Line 9, was aimed at obtaining maximum results with minimum intervention, based on the fundamental conditions for underground construction.
The space is conceived and treated like a "geological" project, respecting the nature of this type of underground location. Materials and construction have a minimalist industrial style since they have been reduced to bare essentials.
The plain industrial design of the elements always used in structural engineering works includes concrete walls, pillars, and prefabricated slab, and in contrast, sheet metal cladding, stone floors, industrial lighting and glass parapets and elevators, as well as the technical equipment necessary for the Barcelona Metro: ticket machines, ticket barriers, information panels.
Natural lighting brings an added quality to these spaces where the great simplicity of design has been much admired, along with the clean lines of the distributive system, scale and dimensions.

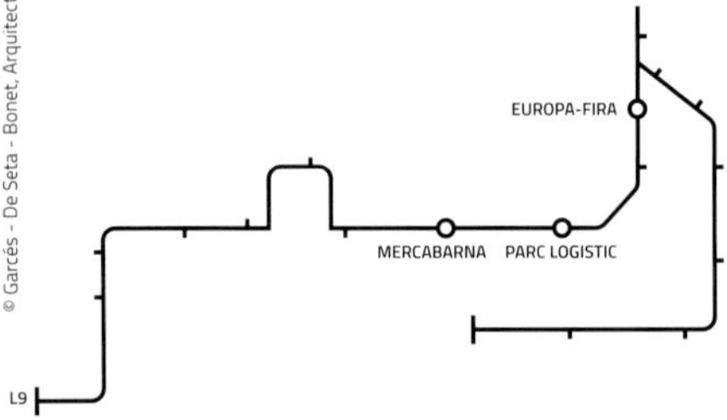

architects
Garcés - De Seta - Bonet, Arquitectes

type
infrastructure

construction
2010 - 2016

52. Hotel Porta Fira

Plaça d'Europa, 45
08908, Barcelona

open to the public

+34 93 233 20 00

www.firabarcelona.com

L9 S > Europa | Fira

As part of the Plaça d'Europa development plan, in 2010 the Japanese architect, Toyo Ito and b720 Arquitectos, designed two 110 metre towers with great impact on the city skyline. The site marks the entrance to the Fira Barcelona Gran Via, one of the largest trade fair complexes in Europe. The project is composed of three distinct, but complementary architectural structures. The first is the low curved building with a Japanese style roof garden that forms the common atrium for access to both towers. The rectangular tower, for office use, defines the physical limit of the Plaça. It features a regular glass curtain façade interrupted by a sinuous red structure to house technical services. The hotel tower has an organic conformation twisting gradually around a central axis. The façade is composed of a double shell with a continuous internal steel skin, covered externally with vertical red aluminium tubes that change direction slightly at each floor level to follow the building's contour.

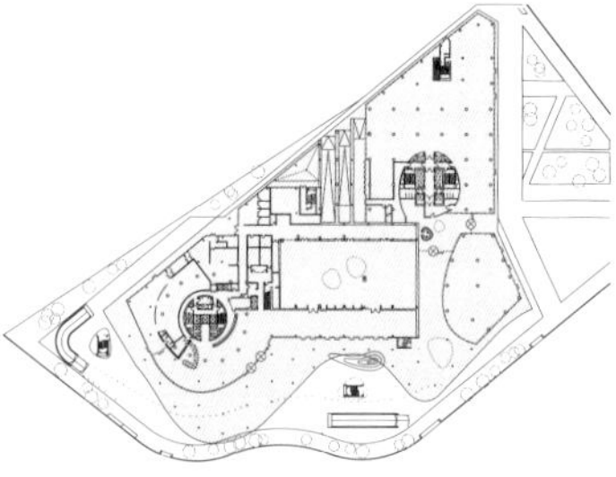

© b720 Fermín Vázquez Arquitectos

architects
b720 Fermín Vázquez Arquitectos; Toyo Ito & Associates, Architects

type
hotel, offices

construction
2010

53. Parc Logístic de la Zona Franca

Avinguda Parc Logístic
08040, Barcelona

open to the public

+34 93 223 91 11
parclogistic@parclogistic.es
www.parclogistic.es

L9 S > Parc Logístic

The Parc Logístic de la Zona Franca is one of the most important service industry centres in the country, and is positioned in a strategic location between the Port of Barcelona and the international Airport. In 2002, the Catalan architect, Ricardo Bofill, designed a complex composed of three separate buildings connected by façade stretching 1.3 kilometres.
Since the site was adjacent to the motorway, extremely high quality materials were required to ensure excellent soundproofing levels within the buildings. The façades all feature a double skin of glass incorporating the latest energy saving systems. They also guarantee maximum natural light into the buildings and permit flexible use of internal space. In 2007, in the same area, Bofill constructed the Abertis Headquarters building for the multinational leader in infrastructural system management. Based on a similar method, the building façade is composed of a glass wall, interrupted by exposed concrete elements to mark each floor level.

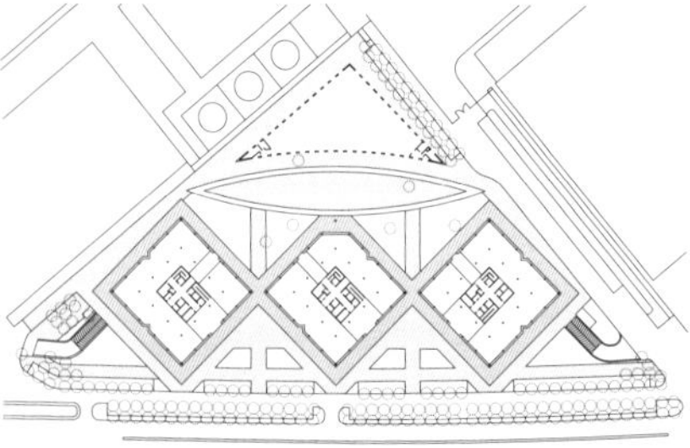

© Ricardo Bofill Taller de Arquitectura

architects
RBTA – Ricardo Bofill
Taller de Arquitectura

type
offices

construction
2002

54. Power plant of Barcelona South / Zona Franca

Carrer Número 27, 6
08040, Barcelona

external viewing only

L9 S > Parc Logístic

Forgas Arquitectes has designed an innovative power plant in the Zona Franca district for power energy transformation and self-generating electricity able to supply a distribution network on an urban scale. As well as the industrial and administrative functions, the design includes an educational space accessible to the public on demand in order to increase public awareness on topics related to environmental sustainability. Visitors can follow a route around the building's perimeter to view the different stages of the productive process from above, followed by a visit to an exhibition space. The tour continues along a walkway incorporated into the façade of the building. Each façade represents an element of the energy production chain (water, biomass, gas) with external cladding in different materials. On one of the façades, a 600 square metre vertical garden has been planted in the metal grid structure to combat industrial CO2 emissions.

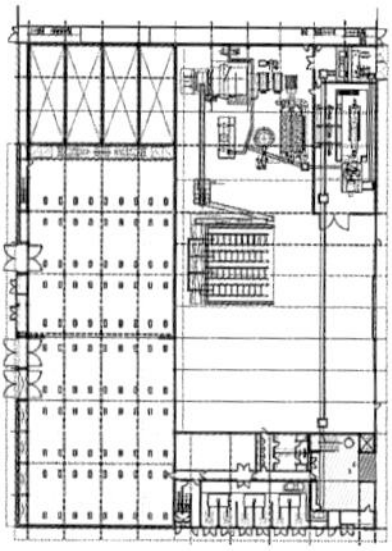

© Forgas Arquitectes

© Simón García | arqfoto.com

architects
Forgas Arquitectes

type
offices

construction
2009 - 2012

55. Parc Esportiu Llobregat

Avinguda del Baix Llobregat
08940, Barcelona

Mon - Sat / 7 am - 10 pm
Sun / 9 am - 2 pm

+34 93 475 35 77
info@parcesportiullobregat.com
www.parcesportiullobregat.com

L5 > Estació de Gavarra

The Cornellà quarter, in the west of Barcelona, is currently organising a public investment program to improve existing infrastructures and services and to build new structures. In 2006, the Portuguese architect Alvaro Siza designed a sports park, almost 10 acres in size, as part of a much larger sports area adjacent to the Llobregat river. The structure is composed of a series of large interconnected buildings housing different sports facilities. A rectangular building houses a sports stadium, an oval structure contains the swimming pool, and auxiliary facilities are housed in an adjacent structure. The buildings are monolithic in style, built in concrete cast on site, a consolidated aspect of Alvaro Siza's work. The indoor pool has an oval dome roof featuring dozens of small round skylights shedding natural light. The pool is connected to a magnificent outdoor pool.

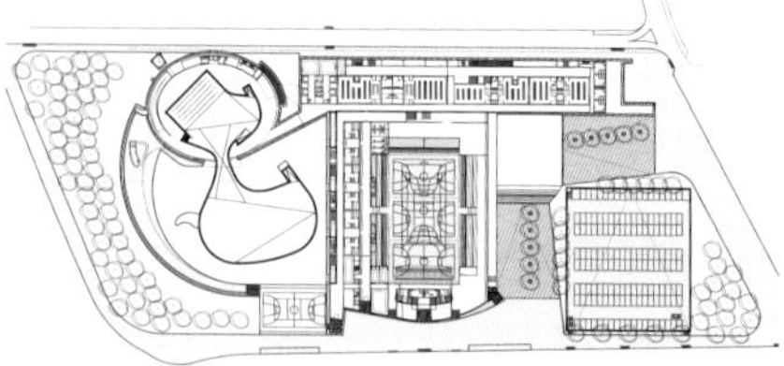

architects
Alvaro Siza

type
sports centre

construction
2006

56. Oficina Registre Civil

Carrer Carles Martí i Vila, 2
08830, Barcelona

Mon - Fri / 9 am - 2 pm
Sat - Sun / closed

+34 93 551 72 35

L8 > Sant Boi

A large number of public buildings have been included in the plan for the expansion of Sant Boi de Llobregat. In 2006, the BAAS architectural firm, based in Barcelona since 1994, designed the Civil Registry building for construction in a newly built square. Three vertical blocks, separated by internal courtyards are set on a common plinth base. Each block performs a different function. To counter the regular geometrical layout, the façade was given dynamic impact by using vertical white concrete staves, interrupted horizontally at each floor. The staves are placed at varying distances from one another and set at different angles to change the perception of the building according to the perspective.

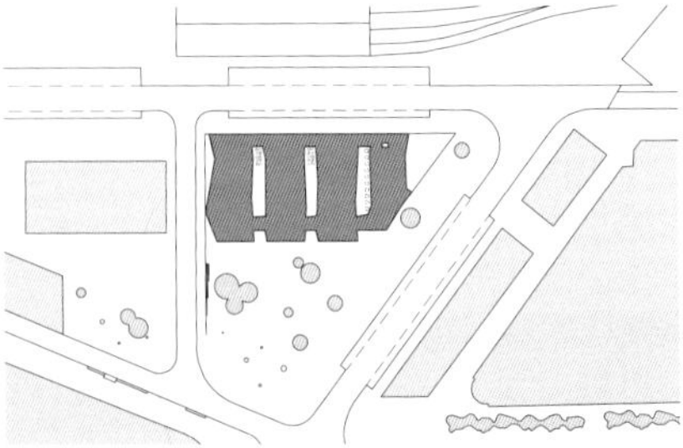

architects
BAAS Arquitectura

type
offices

construction
2002 - 2006

57. Taller de Arquitectura La Fàbrica

Avinguda de la Indústria, 14
08960, Barcelona

Mon - Fri / 10 am - 2 pm,
4 pm - 7 pm
Sat - Sun / closed

+34 93 499 99 00

www.ricardobofill.com

In 1975, Ricardo Bofill converted an abandoned cement factory that dated back to the early years after the war. Today it has become the offices of his architectural firm: Taller de Arquitectura. The architectural reconversion project is the physical demonstration of Bofill's long research towards the negation of functionalism. A process of destroying and transforming existing structures created new functions and relationships between the various parts of the factory. Eight of the thirty silos were reused and now house Bofill's private residence, office space, workshops and archive library, plus a large multifunctional exhibition space called "The Cathedral". The raw exposed concrete and rusted surfaces maintain a strong industrial aesthetic, recalling the original role of the structure. A lush green garden envelopes and covers the whole complex, blurring the line that separates building and vegetation.

L10 / L46 / N12 >
Av. Indústria -
Salvador Espriu

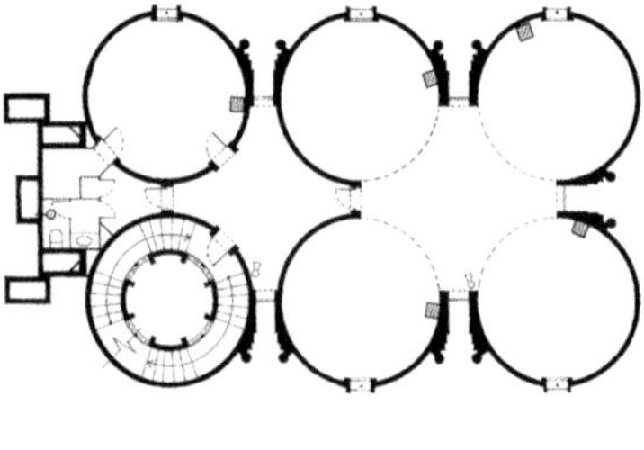

architects
Ricardo Bofill Taller
de Arquitectura

type
architectural office, private
residence, exhibition centre

construction
1975

58. Nexus II

Carrer de Jordi Girona, 2
08034, Barcelona

external viewing only

+34 93 413 77 39

L3 > Palau Reial

Located in the North Campus of the Polytechnic University of Catalonia, Nexus II provides affordable workspace to technology entrepreneurs and start-ups as a business incubator, encouraging experimental technology transfer between the university and business companies. Ricardo Bofill's design is based on total spatial flexibility and strong technological efficiency. It is spread over four floors and the layout is divided into four mutually independent 18×18 meter modular units connected by a central core containing the stairs, accessible from the common hall on the first floor. All floors are open space, in turn divided into modules to provide greater flexibility in planning office layouts. The concrete structure has continuous façades in steel and double glazed windows to insulate and soundproof the interior while allowing natural light to penetrate. The horizontal aspect is highlighted by the use of overhanging roofing that extends on all four sides of the building to protect the interior from direct sunlight.

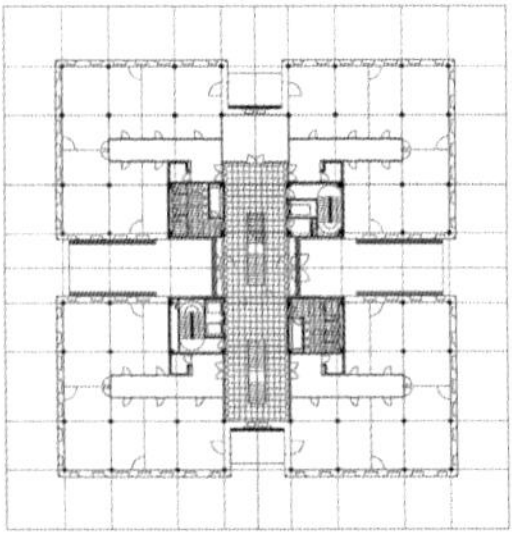

architects
Ricardo Bofill Taller
de Arquitectura

type
offices

construction
2002

59. Centre Cívic Joan Oliver "Pere Quart"

Carrer del Comandant Benítez, 6
08028, Barcelona

Mon - Fri / 9 am - 2 pm,
4 pm - 11 pm
Sat - Sun / 10 am - 2 pm

+34 93 339 82 61
perequart@lleuresport.cat
www.ccperequart.com

L5 > Badal

The Joan Oliver "Pere Quart" civic centre is a municipal public structure in the Les Cortes district for cultural diffusion and the improvement of psychophysical well-being. To increase the number of activities proposed, the size of the building was doubled in 2015, with an additional 900 square metres. The design by Picharchitects is based on the firm's architectural and technological policy of reducing construction time and costs to a minimum, and creating the smallest possible energy and environmental impact.
A new upper floor was added to the main structure using an enveloping light modular metal frame system. The corrugated sheet roofing is self-supporting and echoes the architectural style of the traditional Catalan vault roof. Every element was constructed in a workshop set up on site and assembled during the construction.

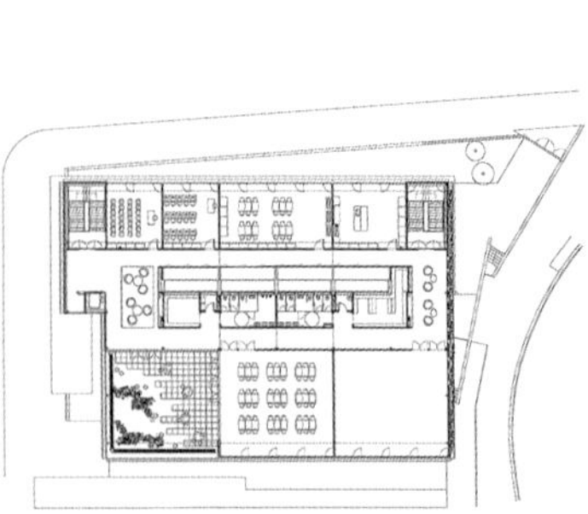

© Picharchitects

architects
Picharchitects
(extension)

type
multi-purpose centre

construction
1999 /
2015 (extension)

60. Roca Barcelona Gallery

Carrer de Joan Güell, 211
08028, Barcelona

Mon - Sat / 10 am - 8 pm
Sun / closed

+34 93 366 12 12

www.rocabarcelonagallery.com

L3 > Les Corts

In 2009, the Carlos Ferrater architectural firm created the first showroom for the Spanish Roca company in the Les Cortes district. Roca is one of the world's leading producers of bathroom fixtures. The building is composed of a compact rectangular box structure, with a glass curtain wall, specifically built by the Spanish company, Cricursa. The main feature of the outer shell is the aquamarine glass panels that de-materialise the surface, refracting the sunlight, and lighting up at night with a system of 4,200 LEDs. The Roca Barcelona Gallery is the first of a series of buildings the company is con structing in major cities in Europe and Asia, commissioned from renowned architectural firms to demonstrate the company's constant research into ecologically sustainable and innovative design.

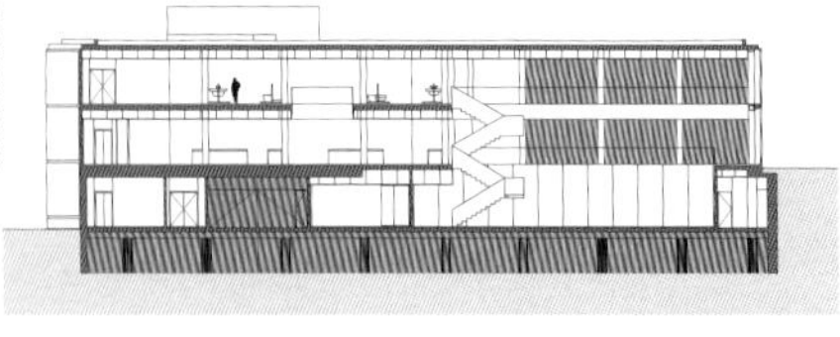

architects
OAB – Office of Architecture in Barcelona (Carlos Ferrater, Borja Ferrater)

type
retail, exhibition centre

construction
2008 - 2009

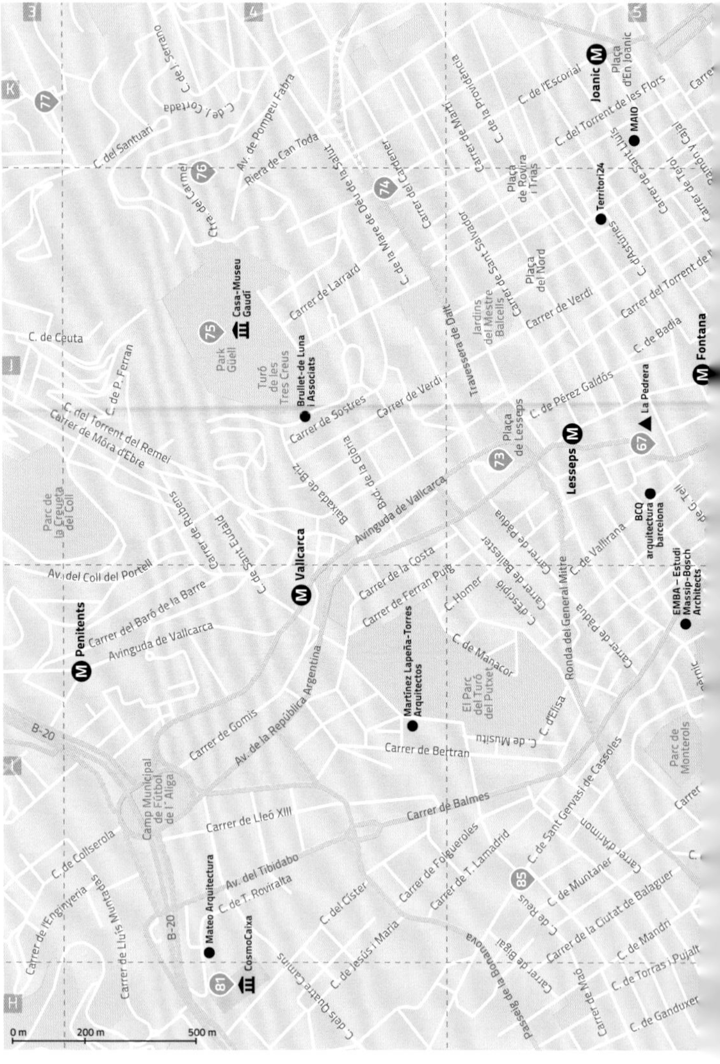

3
4
5
K
J
I
H
77
76
75
74
73
67
81
85
C. de J. Serrano
C. de J. Cortada
C. del Santuari
Av. de Pompeu Fabra
Riera de Can Toda
Ctra. del Carmel
C. de la Mare de Déu de la Salut
Carrer del Cardener
Carrer de Martí
C. de la Providència
C. de l'Escorial
Joanic
Plaça d'En Joanic
C. del Torrent de les Flors
MAIO
Plaça de Rovira i Trias
Territori24
Carrer de Sant Lluís
Carrer de Tigre
Ramon y Cajal
C. d'Astúries
Travessera de Dalt
Carrer de Sant Salvador
Plaça del Nord
Jardins del Mestre Balcells
Carrer de Verdi
Carrer del Torrent de l'Olla
C. de Badia
Fontana
La Pedrera
Casa-Museu Gaudí
Park Güell
Turó de les Tres Creus
Carrer de Larrard
Brullet-de Luna i Associats
Carrer de Sostres
Carrer de Verdi
C. de Ceuta
C. de P. Ferran
C. del Torrent del Remei
Carrer de Móra d'Ebre
Parc de la Creueta del Coll
Carrer de Rubens
C. de Sant Eudald
Baixada de Briz
Bxd. de la Glòria
Avinguda de Vallcarca
Plaça de Lesseps
C. de Pérez Galdós
Lesseps
BCQ arquitectura barcelona
C. de Vallirana
Carrer de Pàdua
Carrer de Ballester
C. d'Escipió
Av. del Coll del Portell
Vallcarca
Carrer de la Costa
Carrer de Ferran Puig
C. Homer
EMBA – Estudi Massip-Bosch Architects
Ronda del General Mitre
Carrer del Baró de la Barre
Penitents
Avinguda de Vallcarca
C. de Manacor
Martínez Lapeña-Torres Arquitectos
El Parc del Turó del Putxet
C. d'Elisa
Av. de la República Argentina
Carrer de Gomis
C. de Musitu
Carrer de Bertran
B-20
Camp Municipal de Fútbol de l' Àliga
Carrer de Lleó XIII
Carrer de Balmes
C. de Sant Gervasi de Cassoles
Parc de Monterols
C. de Collserola
Carrer de l'Enginyeria
Carrer de Lluís Muntadas
Av. del Tibidabo
C. de T. Roviralta
Mateo Arquitectura
CosmoCaixa
C. del Císter
Carrer de Folgueroles
Carrer de T. Lamadrid
Carrer d'Arimon
C. de Muntaner
C. de Reus
Carrer de la Ciutat de Balaguer
C. de Mandri
C. de Torras i Pujalt
C. de Ganduxer
Carrer de Maó
Carrer de Bigai
Passeig de la Bonanova
C. de Jesús i Maria
C. dels Quatre Camins
0 m
200 m
500 m

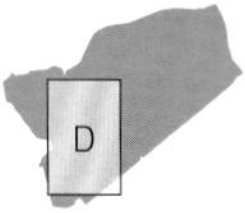

Eixample – Gracia – Sants – Sarrià

61. Centre Cívic Cristalleries Planell
62. El Fil Nursery
63. Centre Cívic Urgell
64. Mercat del Ninot
65. 110 Rooms
66. Fundació Antoni Tàpies
67. Casa Vicens – Casa Batlló – Casa Milà "La Pedrera"
68. Suite Avenue
69. Sagrada Familia
70. Biblioteca Vila de Gràcia
71. Col·legi d'Economistes de Catalunya
72. Vil·la Urània
73. Biblioteca Jaume Fuster
74. Santa Madrona Dwellings
75. Park Güell
76. Centre Esportiu Municipal Can Toda
77. Turó de La Rovira
78. Fabra i Coats – Fàbrica de Creació de Barcelona
79. Centre Cívic Baró de Viver
80. Torre Júlia
81. CosmoCaixa Barcelona
82. Torre de Collserola
83. Oak House School
84. Lycée Français Maternelle
85. Biblioteca Sant Gervasi – Joan Maragall
86. Col·legi Major Sant Jordi

61. Centre Cívic Cristalleries Planell

Carrer del Dr. Ibáñez, 38
08014, Barcelona

open to the public

L3 > Les Corts

The Cristalleries Planell factory, famous for its glass production, was built in 1913 on a small triangular site in the historic quarter of Les Corts. Today the site hosts a striking red brick multifunctional public complex.
The restoration project by Harquitectes was awarded several international prizes and is a sign of the firm's constant research into architectural conservation and environmental sustainability. The key element of the project is a narrow rectangular courtyard, created by recessing the new building in relation to the southern façade which is subject to heritage building restrictions. The courtyard is the meeting point of two architectural periods and creates the link with the contemporary building. The empty space also functions as an internal micro-climate: the connection between the courtyard, patio on the northern roof and four glazed rooftop chimneys makes maximum use of natural light, spreading it to all four floors, and using the physical function of the "Venturi effect", the space also performs a natural air recycling action.

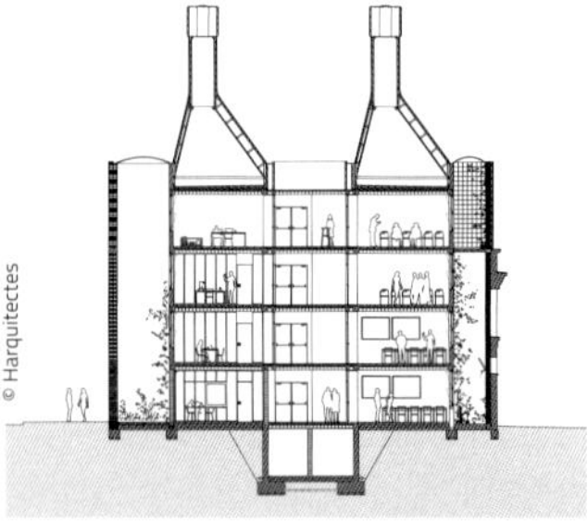

© Harquitectes

© Adrià Goula

architects
Josep Graner i Prat / Harquitectes (extension and restoration)

type
multi-purpose complex

construction
1913 / 2016 (extension and restoration)

62. El Fil Nursery

Carrer de Robrenyo, 81
08002, Barcelona

open to the public

L3 > Plaça del Centre
L3 / L5 > Sants Estació

The recent restoration and development plan for the Jardins de Màlaga resulted in assigning a small site for the construction of a local nursery school, designed in 2010 by Catalan architects Battle i Roig. The building is composed of two superposed rectangular blocks, with a projected cantilever over the entrance creating a small covered area. The southern-facing exposure provides maximum natural sunlight in the classrooms which are accessed from a wide corridor with a glazed wall opening onto a side patio. The exterior is designed as a monolithic block with a uniform colour palette, both for the exposed concrete structure and the continuous perforated metal panel façades. In sharp contrast, the interior is filled with light, and decorated with vibrant colours. Interior furnishings are in tactile materials such as rubber and wood.

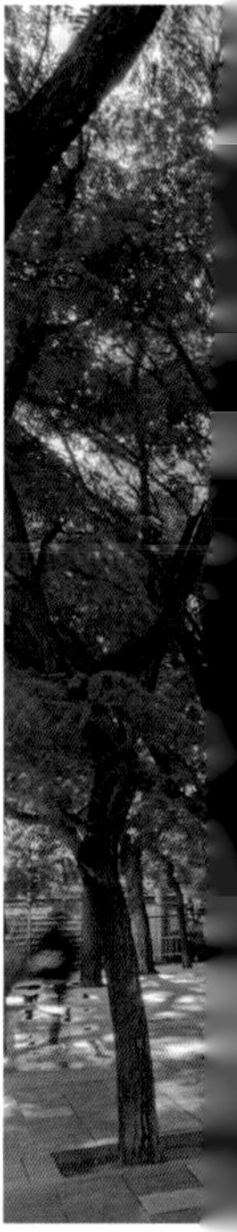

© Batlle i Roig Arquitectura

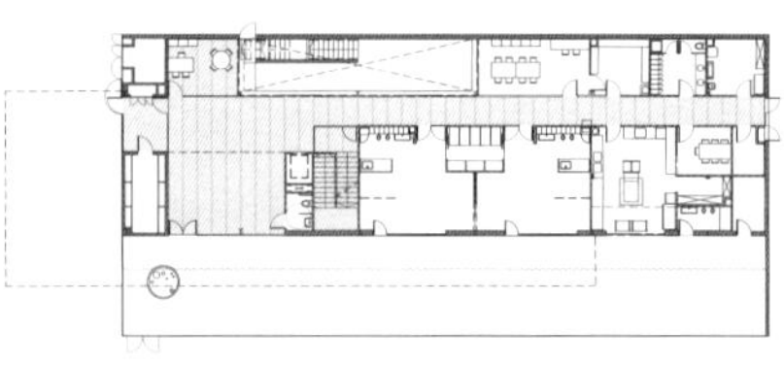

architects
Batlle i Roig Arquitectura

type
school

construction
2011

63. Centre Cívic Urgell

Carrer Comte d'Urgell, 145
08036, Barcelona

Mon - Fri / 9 am - 9 pm
Sat / 10 am - 2 pm,
4 pm - 8 pm
Sun / closed

+34 93 453 64 80
info@ccurgell.cat
www.ccurgell.cat

L5 > Hospital Clínic

The architects, Víctor Rahola and Jorge Vidal, have designed a multifunctional building with a surprising variety of spatial and architectural solutions in the heart of the compact urban Eixample landscape. Seen from Carrer Comte d'Urgell, the so-called "collage building" appears to be a solid glass and concrete building, but on entering the internal courtyard of the site, the structural layout is very striking. Five different public services are grouped in a vertical block overlooking a small public park. The building is composed of a horizontal structure with a different layout on each floor with different internal spaces, double height areas, loggias, internal gardens, and play areas. The structure features a wide range of different colours and construction materials. An interesting element is the small auditorium whose curving profile contrasts with the straight lines of the internal façade.

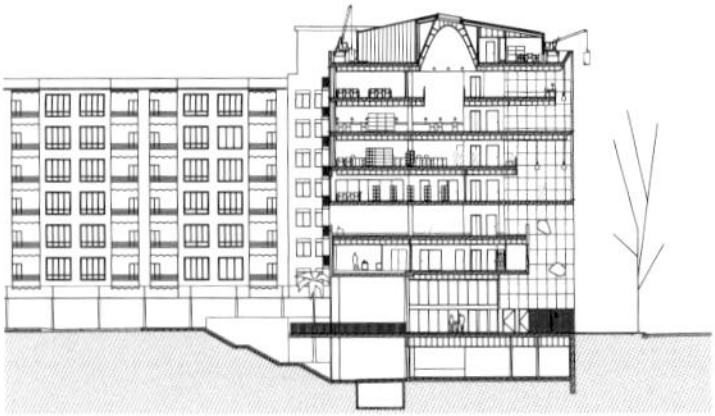

© Víctor Rahola Arquitecte

architects
Víctor Rahola, Jorge Vidal

type
multi-purpose complex

construction
2011

64. Mercat del Ninot

Carrer de Mallorca, 133
08036, Barcelona

Mon - Sat / 8 am - 9.30 pm
Sun / closed

+34 93 323 49 09
info@mercatdelninot.com
www.mercatdelninot.com

L5 > Hospital Clínic

One of the most recent reconstruction projects for the markets of Barcelona, traditional spaces for socialising and buying fresh produce, has been the old iron and glass structure of the Mercat del Ninot (1889), based on the project by Josep Lluís Mateo. The building stands out in the midst of the surrounding streets because of the high tech, adjustable, metal louvre shutters that cover all the windows to full height along the entire perimeter of the building. They prevent the sun from penetrating the building and damaging the produce. Apart from the shutter system, the shell and external structure were preserved and restored so that the effect seen from the street is that of its original form. A further level was excavated underground to house a supermarket. According to the designer: "Since they were invented, markets have always resembled large covered squares", and the interior echoes an urban system of streets and open spaces that become not simply a thoroughfare, but also a place to meet and socialise.

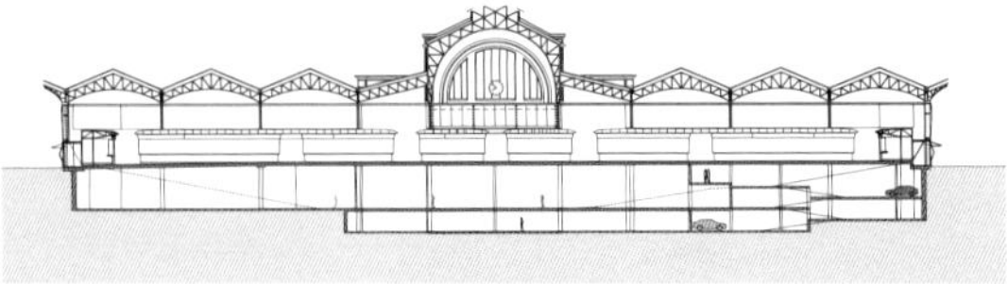

architects
Mateo Arquitectura

type
retail

construction
2015

65. 110 Rooms

Carrer de Provença, 203
08008, Barcelona

external viewing only

L6 / L7 > Provença

Laid out over five floors, this residential building is unusual for the innovative style of its apartments. No precedence has been given to any particular space as all rooms are identical in size, opening onto one another without corridors or hallways. The standard apartments are composed of five single rooms which can be expanded or reduced according to needs, to become living rooms, dining rooms or bedrooms. To provide this flexibility, the kitchen and bathroom blocks are strategically placed at the centre of each apartment. Air and light are spread equally among all the rooms thanks to an internal courtyard space, ideal for natural ventilation. This innovative approach is based on an old traditional style, reinventing the concept that existed in 19th century Eixample architecture, composed of standard units, similar in size and shape, that permitted easy modification and change in purpose over time. The same concept applies to the entrance, typical of Eixample housing, where the space was designed to perform a variety of functions. Here it has been reinvented as a lobby with the daring impact of an art installation.

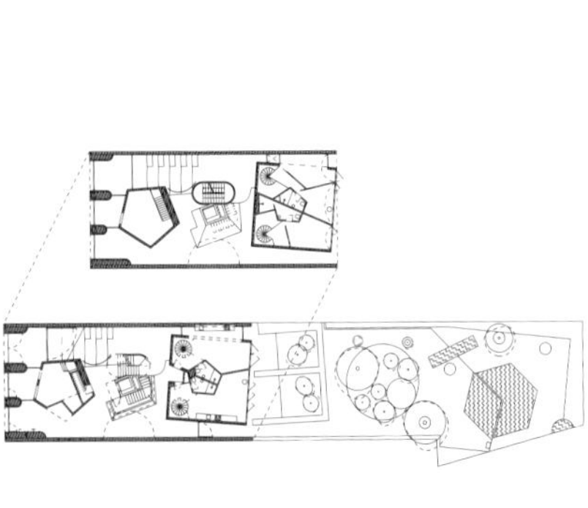

architects
MAIO

type
residential

construction
2016

66. Fundació Antoni Tàpies

Carrer d'Aragó, 55
08007, Barcelona

Mon / closed
Tue - Thu, Sat /
10 am - 7 pm
Fri / 10 am - 9 pm
Sun / 10 am - 3 pm

+34 93 487 03 15

www.fundaciotapies.org

L3 / L5 > Diagonal

Located in the Eixample district, the Fundació Antoni Tàpies is a fine example of the avant-garde architecture of the early Catalan Modernist period, as well as being home to the main collection of one of the greatest Catalan artists of the 20th century. Designed in 1884 by the Modernist architect, Lluís Domènech i Montaner for a publishing house, the building combines an exposed iron structure with a red brick façade decorated with Islamic inspired motifs and large Art Nouveau windows. Antoni Tàpies, whose artistic experimentation had a strong political impact during the period under Franco, set up a foundation in 1984 to promote contemporary Catalan art, and included 800 of his own works. His huge sculpture, *Nuvol i Cadira* [Cloud and Chair] has become the emblem of the foundation. The building was recently restored and extended to create further exhibition spaces, moving the administration office spaces to three new underground floors, accessible from the internal courtyard.

© Ábalos + Sentkiewicz

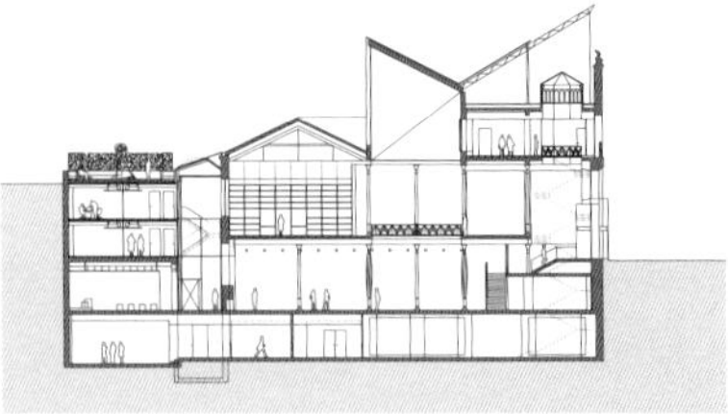

architects
Lluís Domènech i Montaner / Ábalos + Sentkiewicz (restoration)

type
museum, cultural centre

construction
1884 / 2009 (restoration)

67. Casa Vicens – Casa Batlló – Casa Milà "La Pedrera"

Casa Vicens:
Carrer de les Carolines, 20-26
08012, Barcelona
Casa Batlló:
Passeig de Gràcia, 43
08007, Barcelona
"La Pedrera":
Passeig de Gràcia, 92
08008, Barcelona

Casa Vicens:
Mon / 10 am - 3 pm
Tue - Sun / 10 am - 7 pm
Casa Batlló:
Mon - Sun / 9 am - 9 pm
"La Pedrera":
Summer and Christmas /
Mon - Sun / 9 am - 8.30 pm,
9 pm - 11 pm
Winter / Mon - Sun / 9 am -
6.30 pm, 7 pm - 9 pm

Casa Vicens: +34 93 54759 80
Casa Batlló: +34 93 2160306
"La Pedrera": +34 93 2142576

casavicens.org
www.casabatllo.es
www.lapedrera.com

L3 / L5 > Diagonal

Between the 19th and 20th centuries, Barcelona underwent a large demographic boom which led to the creation of the brand new quarter called Eixample (literal translation: "enlargement"), established in the famous urban plan designed by Ildefons Cerdà. A large number of middle-class houses were built, principally located along and around the Passeig de Gràcia, the main 19th century road between Barcelona and the small town of Gràcia. In 1878, fresh from university, the young Antoni Gaudí designed his first house, Casa Vicens. This residence, which was recently restored by Martínez Lapeña-Torres Arquitectos, materialises his concept of strong structural expression, in a blend of Catalan revival and Islamic-Mediterranean styles. In 1904, when restoring Casa Batlló, he experimented with a more organic style that resulted in the sculpted façade in Montjuïc limestone and decorated with tessera in multicoloured ceramics. Later, the massive undulating stone profile of "La Pedrera" emerged in the midst of the compact order of the neighbourhood. Gaudí concealed the structural system but maintained his strong expressive quality.

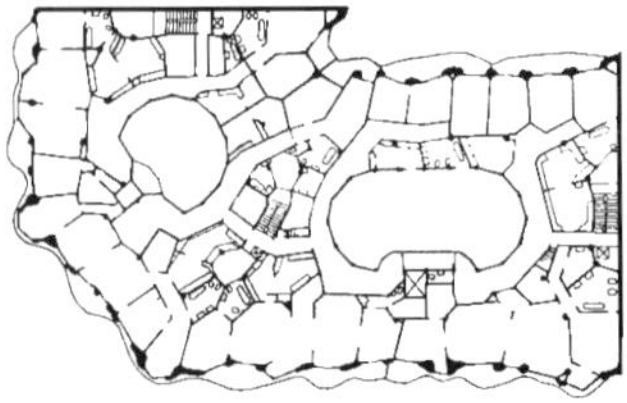

© Catalunya La Pedrera Foundation

architects
Antoni Gaudí

type
museum, residential

construction
Casa Vicens: 1888
Casa Batlló: 1904 -1906
"La Pedrera": 1906 - 1912

68. Suite Avenue

Passeig de Gràcia, 83
08008, Barcelona

open to the public

+34 93 487 41 59

www.suitesavenue.com

L3 / L5 > Diagonal

In 2009, the Japanese architectural firm Toyo Ito & Associates, Architects was commissioned to design the front façade and the internal façade facing the sunlit courtyard of an office building in the Passeig de Gràcia, to be renovated into a luxury residence with 41 apartments. Without modifying the curtain wall structure of the building, it was clad with a new sculptural façade composed of sheet metal waving lines, a homage to Gaudí's Pedrera, not far away. The material's mother of pearl surface emphasises the organic atmosphere of the façade reflecting the sunlight. The building's central core, patios, and internal spaces were designed by the Spanish architects Carlos Basso and Toni Olaya. The rooms are decorated with fine art works, and on the ground floor, an exhibition space houses archaeological pieces from the Clos Foundation, examples of traditional Hindu art from the 14th and 19th centuries.

© Toyo Ito & Associates, Architects

architects
Toyo Ito & Associates, Architects

type
hotel

construction
2009

69. Sagrada Familia

Carrer de Mallorca, 401
08013, Barcelona

November - February
Mon - Sun / 9 am - 8 pm
March
Mon - Sun / 9 am - 7 pm
April - September
Mon - Sun / 9 am - 8 pm
October
Mon - Sun / 9 am - 7 pm

25 - 26 December, 1st and 6th January / 9 am - 2 pm

+34 93 208 04 14
informacio@sagradafamilia.org.
www.sagradafamilia.org

L4 / L5 > Verdaguer

Antoni Gaudí worked intensely on the Sagrada Familia throughout his whole career, and it is now the most visited monument in all of Spain. The masterpiece, still under construction over a century later, was initially financed by the Spiritual Association of Devotees of Saint Joseph that commissioned an Expiatory Temple in Neo-Gothic style from Francisco de Paula, but was later taken over by Gaudí, almost by accident. The initial project was changed completely, but the cathedral maintained the traditional Latin cross layout with a transept and seven apse chapels, embracing an organic style, but which remained Gothic in its main structure. The cathedral is famous for its powerfully upward thrusting design, terminating externally in pinnacles, towers and peaks. The project, 70% finished now, envisaged three richly decorated façades showing the different stages of the life of Jesus: birth, passion, and glory. The interior is based on the concept of a forest, with high columns in tree form and branch-like ribbing that supports the complex structure of the steeply curved vaulted ceilings.

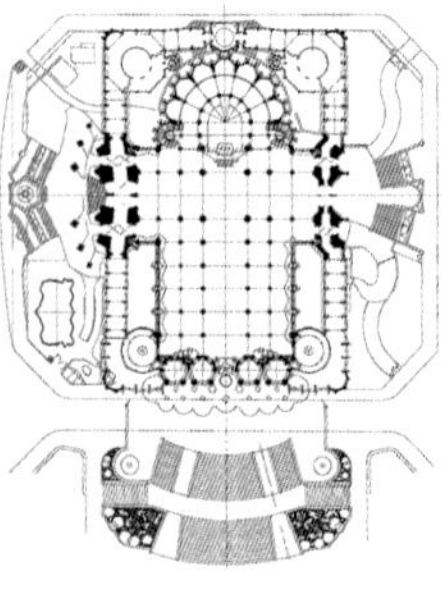

architects
Antoni Gaudí

type
church

construction
1882 - under construction

70. Biblioteca Vila de Gràcia

Carrer del Torrent de l'Olla, 104
08012, Barcelona

Mon, Wed - Thu / 10 am - 8 pm
Tue, Fri / 10 am - 2 pm, 4 pm - 9 pm
Sat - Sun / closed

+34 93 284 77 90

www.barcelona.cat

L3 > Fontana

The library is located on the corner of an intersection that forms the contact point between the Gràcia quarter and the city. The shape and size of the plot is typical of residential building plots in the area, but was apparently not practical for public structures. This proved to be the main restraint when designing the building. The fact that the "container" and "content" do not coincide, is clearly expressed in the façades where enlarged and expanded elements have been incorporated to varying degrees as a system to express the importance and exceptional nature of the internal functions. "Like a suitcase that is deformed when you add more than it can contain", explains Llinàs.
The building is composed of 4 floors plus a basement level, and is designed with a vertical concept, unusual for a library. The ground floor houses the lending library and hemeroteca. The second floor is the children's section, and the upper floors house a general public area, reading rooms, offices, and work spaces. Different sections, both internal and external, have been decorated using a fascinating blend of random letters from various Mediterranean languages, both ancient and modern.

© Josep Llinàs

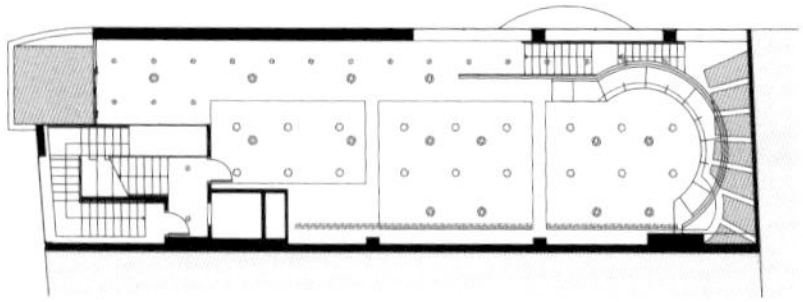

architects
Josep Llinàs

type
library

construction
2002

71. Col·legi d'Economistes de Catalunya

Plaça Gal·la Placídia, 32
08006, Barcelona

Mon - Thu / 9 am - 7 pm
Fri / 8 am - 3 pm
Sat - Sun / closed

+34 93 416 16 04
cec@coleconomistes.cat
www.coleconomistes.cat

L3 > Fontana

On the edge of the Gràcia and Sarrià-Sant Gervasi neighbourhoods, the new Catalan Institute of Economists occupies a 32 metre-long site that terminates in the Plaça Gal·la Placídia, which will also form part of the project intervention. This new building is composed of a steel structure with double glazed uniform façade on south side. The entrance foyers, waiting areas, and circulation routes on various levels follow an identical layout, and are all arranged along the lengthwise façades in direct contact with the Plaça. The modular panels on the façades are plain white glass, transparent, translucent, or opaque, according to lighting necessities. The internal layout is composed of six structural blocks of various dimensions and shapes, positioned at different heights and clad in glass, steel or wood according to functional needs.

© Roldán + Berengué

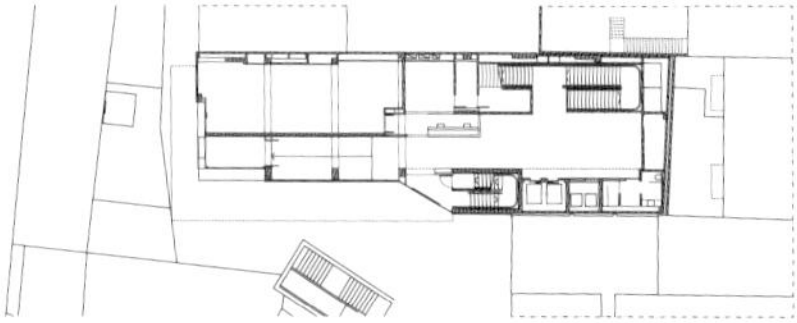

architects
Roldán + Berengué

type
office

construction
2013

72. Vil·la Urània

Via Augusta, 102
08006, Barcelona

open to the public

L3 > Fontana

Vil·la Urània is a small residence built in the late 19th century, located in the Sarrià-Sant Gervasi district; it was formerly the home of the famous astronomer, Josep Comas y Solà. Urban densification in this area, previously a garden-city, has left this building and its garden squeezed between two tall blind walls. The project is aimed at recovering the villa for use as a multi-function space and at creating a new building that will be extended to house a social centre, a children's home and exhibition spaces. This new building features a long gallery that provides passive cooling and heating in corridors and informal socialising areas. In winter it will act as a greenhouse, and in summer, as a pergola, creating thermal protection to reduce the energy requirements of the complex, making the building almost completely self-sufficient. Different layered filters adapted to the external conditions are the basis for a green planted façade, compatible with the activities of the building's users. All materials used are renewable, can be recycled and have low environmental impact.

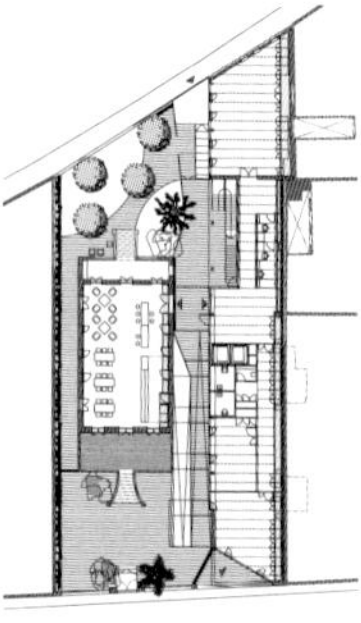

© SUMO Arquitectes

architects
SUMO Arquitectes,
Yolanda Olmo

type
public facility

construction
2017

73. Biblioteca Jaume Fuster

Plaça de Lesseps, 20-22
08023, Barcelona

Tue - Fri / 10 am - 9 pm
Mon - Sat / 10 am - 2 pm,
4 pm - 9 pm
Sun / 11 am - 2 pm

+34 93 368 45 64

ajuntament.barcelona.cat

L3 > Lesseps

The Plaça de Lesseps, on the border between the Gràcia and Sarrià-Sant Gervasi districts, is one of the busiest traffic areas in Barcelona. Since 2000, the area has undergone numerous interventions to improve traffic conditions and the new urban planning scheme established the inclusion of a municipal library dedicated to the Catalan writer Jaume Fuster. The project was designed by Josep Llinas and Joan Vera and has been awarded numerous prizes including the prestigious FAD Architecture Prize in 2016. The library has a complex structure based on a rhombus shaped layout. The roof slopes in various directions and projects over the three main façades creating covered areas faced in wood. The 5,026 square metre interior is spread over four floors and includes an auditorium, a multimedia room and a large exhibition space.

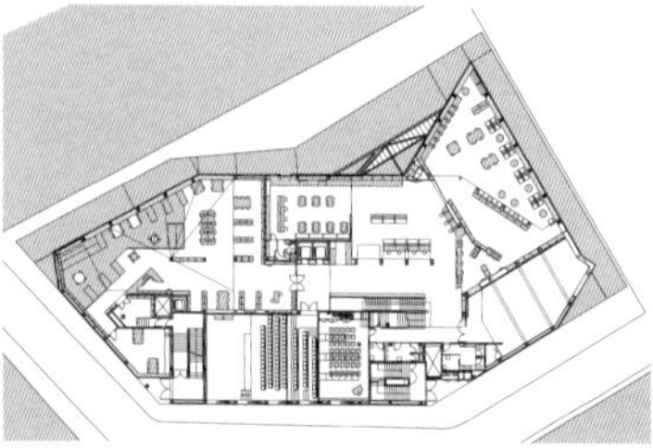

© Josep Llinás

architects
Josep Llinas, Joan Vera

type
library

construction
2005

74. Santa Madrona Dwellings

Travessera de Dalt, 92
08024, Barcelona

external viewing only

L3 > Lesseps
L4 > Alfons X | Joanic

In 2013, Picharchitects designed a small square containing two low cost apartment building in an urban block in the long Travessera de Dalt, with public financing and the help of the Obra Social la Caixa. The project is part of the architects' consolidated concept which they call "circular economy", aimed at urban and construction design with a strong focus on economic, environmental, and social sustainability. The Santa Madrona Dwellings stand out in the neighbourhood for their coloured balconies and chequerboard surface cladding. The structure is based on bearing walls using locally produced industrialised construction systems. The internal layout applies contemporary bioclimatic parameters, which provide a drastic reduction in energy requirements in the apartment buildings, supplied exclusively by renewable energy systems.

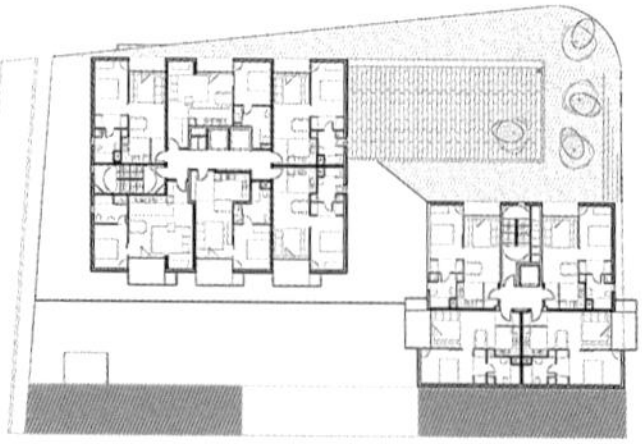

architects
Picharchitects

type
residential

construction
2013

75. Park Güell

Carrer d'Olot
08024, Barcelona

28 October - 17 February
Mon - Sun / 8.30 am - 6.15 pm
17 February - 24 March
Mon - Sun / 8.30 am - 7.00 pm
25 March - 29 April
Mon - Sun / 8 am - 8.30 pm
30 April - 26 August
Mon - Sun / 8 am - 9.30 pm
27 August - 27 October
Mon - Sun / 8 am - 8.30 pm

+34 93 409 18 31

www.parkguell.cat

L3 > Vallcarca | Lesseps

The Park Güell dates from Antoni Gaudí's early architectural career, and is closely linked with Eusebi Güell, an industrialist with strongly progressive ideas. It is the uncompleted project for a wealthy class garden-city in a zone that underwent urban expansion in the early 20th century. (Gràcia was not incorporated into Barcelona until 1897). The Park was opened to the public in 1926 and is integrated into the undulating landscape of the Carmel Hill. Two pavillions next to the entrance, the porter's lodge and the reception, were inspired by the opera "Hansel and Gretel" played at the Liceu Theatre in Barcelona, in between 1900-1901 and lead to the iconic double stairway with its mosaic decorations and the salamander which has become of the most famous symbols of the city. From here, the route continues to the Hypostyle Room, originally designed as a market for the estate, featuring 86 columns with a dual function: a support structure and as a rainwater drainage system. A large area has remained as a tree-planted park, but numerous pathways and panoramic viewpoints were also constructed, including the Turó de les Tres Creus which marks the highest point in the park.

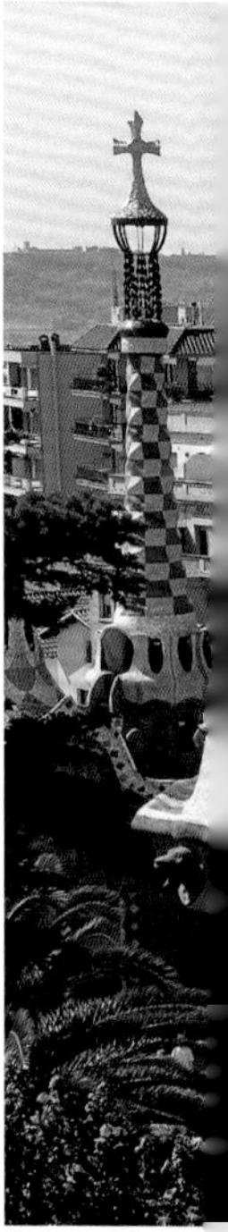

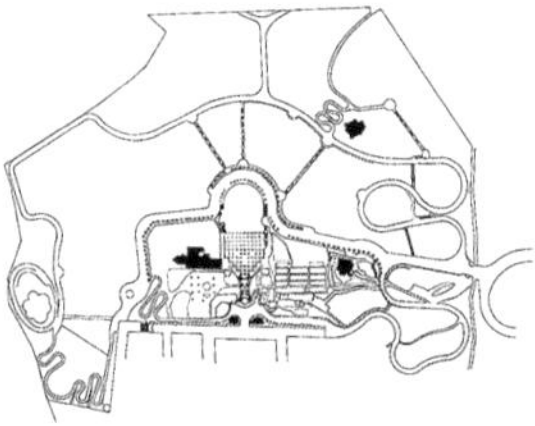

architects
Antoni Gaudí

type
park

construction
1900 - 1914

76. Centre Esportiu Municipal Can Toda

Carrer de Ramiro de Maeztu, 25
08024, Barcelona

Mon - Fri / 6.45 am - 11 pm
Sat / 7 am - 9.30 pm
Sun / 7 am - 3 pm

+34 93 213 43 44

www.cncatalunya.cat

L4 > Alfons X

The Centre Esportiu Municipal Can Toda has hosted the Catalan Swimming Club on the Carmel Hill since the 1970s. The club is renowned for its swimming and water polo teams. Founded in the Barceloneta quarter in 1931, the club reached its peak in the 1990s, and was transferred to a larger and more functional sports centre in the Gràcia district. In 2006, the CNC commissioned the Catalan architectural firm, AIA Salazar Navarro, to update and extend the current facilities to cater for a larger public and improve the architectural style. The architects have long experience in working on numerous similar projects for sports centres, with a strong focus on sustainability, technology, and efficiency. The project for the Can Toda sports centre involved widespread reorganisation of the structure and space layout, as well as incorporating innovative technology for air and water temperature control throughout the entire complex.

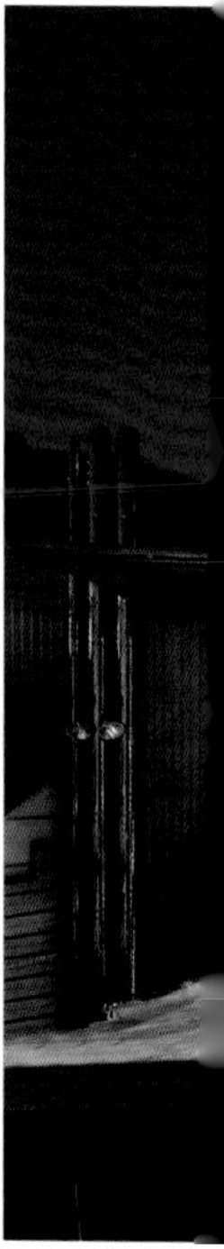

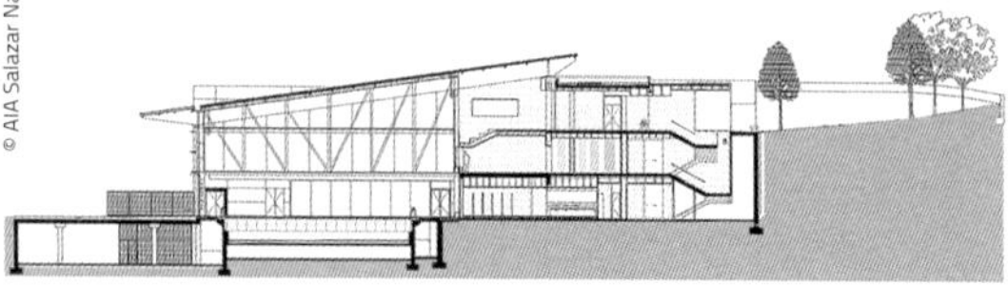

architects
AIA Salazar Navarro

type
sports centre

construction
2010

77. Turó de La Rovira

Carrer de Marià Labèrnia
08032, Barcelona

open to the public

www.bunkers.cat

L4 > Alfons X

At a height of 262 metres, Turó de La Rovira offers the most extensive views over the whole of Barcelona. Used as an anti-aircraft battery emplacement during World War II, it was later occupied by about 100 illegal dwellings that were cleared and dismantled before the Olympics. The zone was rendered usable again in 2011 after careful restoration work by the architects, Jansana, de la Villa, de Paauw and Jordi Romero, specialised in urban scale landscape interventions. The aim of the project was to keep intervention to a minimum in order to restore the area as a historical site, preserving the multiple architectural layers as far as possible. Turó de La Rovira is an archaeological space that includes traces of World War II, the self-constructed habitations that grew spontaneously over the 20th century, and the evolution of Barcelona's urban fabric heritage. The project was awarded the European Prize for Urban Public Space 2012 for "its rarity and originality in terms of protection of the immaterial heritage".

© Jansana, de la Villa, de Paauw, arquitectes

architects
Jansana, de la Villa, de Paauw, arquitectes; AAUP, arquitectes (restoration)

type
park

construction
2011 (restoration)

78. Fabra i Coats – Fàbrica de Creació de Barcelona

Carrer Sant Adrià, 20
08030, Barcelona

Mon - Fri / 9 am - 10 pm
Sat / 10 am - 8.30 pm
Sun / closed

+34 93 256 61 50

fabraicoats.bcn.cat

L1 > Sant Andreu

The Fabra i Coats factory was built in 1910 in the historic quarter of Sant Andreu, which was not integrated with Barcelona until the end of the 19th century. The complex is composed of three separate adjacent buildings, converted in 2012 to provide a multifunctional structure for artistic creation with a multidisciplinary art school and exhibition spaces. The project strategy was aimed at respecting the original structural and constructive elements of the internal space in order to cater for the school's complex functional program. The building is based on a modular system of steel pillars to create open space areas and complete internal distribution flexibility. The technological components and service systems are enclosed in special vertical shafts. The open spaces can be divided using mobile cable and sail partitions to create separate private areas of different dimensions according to necessity.

© Ruisánchez Arquitectes

architects
Manuel Ruisánchez,
Francesc Bacardit

type
multi-purpose complex

construction
2012

79. Centre Cívic Baró de Viver

Carrer de Quito, 8
08030, Barcelona

Mon - Fri / 10 am - 2.30 pm,
4 pm - 9.30 pm
Sat / 10 am - 2 pm,
4 pm - 8 pm
Sun / closed

+34 93 256 50 97

L1 > Baró de Viver

The Centre Cívic Baró de Viver is an interesting multi-functional public structure located in an area on the northern edge of Barcelona, and was designed to improve the community life of the local neighbourhood. With a 40×40 metre floor plan, the building was constructed with a low-tech design approach using a prefabricated concrete structural system for the framework to save on building costs and construction time. The modular pillar system provides great flexibility for internal spaces as they can be easily modified for any possible future changes or needs. The façade is composed of a double skin with a layer of prefabricated panels that incorporate electrical and plumbing systems, and an external system composed of a modular tubular steel protection. Great attention was paid to energy efficiency: natural light in all spaces is combined with lighting powered by solar panels. All irrigation and sanitary water is provided by recycled rainwater. It is the first LEED Platinum NC building of Catalonia.

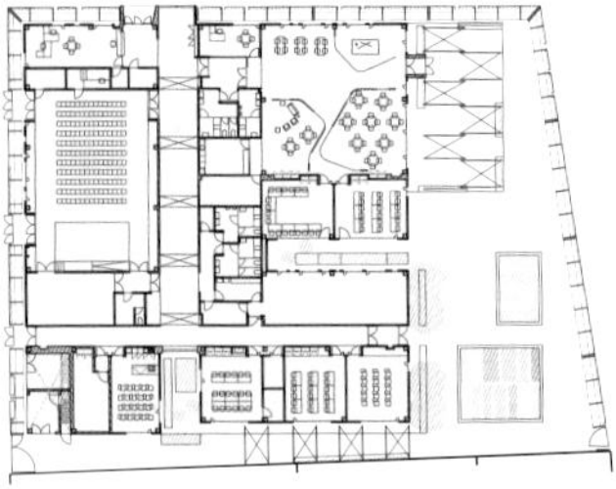

© Territori24

architects
Territori24

type
multi-purpose complex

construction
2014

80. Torre Júlia

Via Favència, 348
08016, Barcelona

external viewing only

L4 > Via Júlia

Torre Júlia has become a dominant feature on the skyline in the northern suburbs of Barcelona. Seventeen storeys high, this square block building was designed as social housing for the elderly, and completes the urban plan of the area adjacent to Ronda del Litoral, an artery road introduced in 1992. The building is unusual for its double layer façade with internal surfaces painted in different colours to divide the block into three sections. The white concrete external layer is composed of deep balconies and stairways leading up to roof level. The horizontal elements have been designed like a structural cantilevered system and form a linear internal corridor with views over the city. Each section has a double height common area for socialising and collective activities. Even the roof can be used by the inhabitants. It has been organised as a furnished garden with panoramic views, while at street level, there is a sports centre for the local community.

architects
Pau Vidal, Sergi Pons architects, Ricard Galiana

type
residential

construction
2011

81. CosmoCaixa Barcelona

Carrer d'Isaac Newton, 26
08022, Barcelona

Mon - Sun / 10 am - 8 pm

+34 93 212 60 50

www.cosmocaixa.com

L3 > Penitents

Set in the midst of private residences on the slopes of the Tibidabo Hills, the new CosmoCaixa science museum is one of the most popular attractions in Barcelona. This part of the museum was built recently, while the building hosting other exhibitions dates back to 1909. The new construction has an innovative educational concept aimed at encouraging visitors to interact constantly with the museum spaces. The project designed by Terradas Arquitectos in 2004, covers a total area of almost 50 thousand square metres, divided into six sections according to different subjects, plus two temporary exhibition areas. The most famous exhibition space is the Amazon forest planted in a glass-house and including native flora and fauna. The architectural design features a modular structure, with a helical staircase in the centre of the building that connects all nine floors of the museum, six of which are underground. The staircase creates a light well for the entire museum.

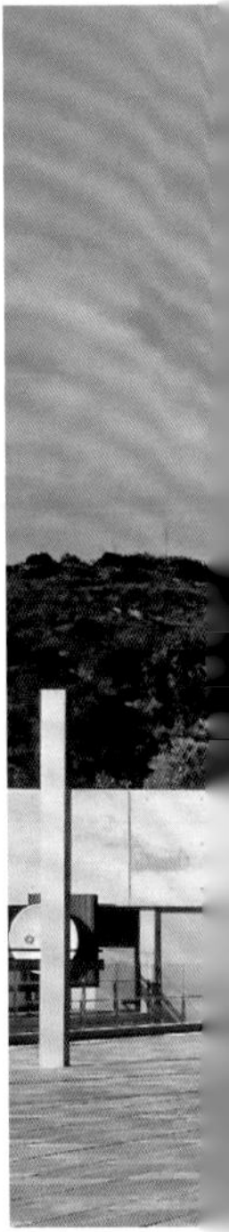

© Terradas Arquitectos

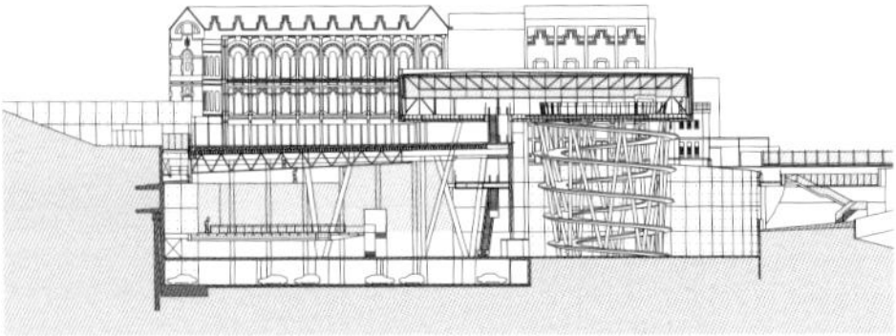

architects
Terradas Arquitectos

type
museum

construction
2004

82. Torre de Collserola

Carretera de Vallvidrera al Tibidabo
08017, Barcelona

Mon - Fri / closed
Sat - Sun / 12 pm - 1.45 pm, 3.30 pm - 7.45 pm

+34 93 406 93 54

www.torredecollserola.com

111 > Accés Escola Judicial

Four Olympic sports areas were created in different areas of the city for the 1992 Olympic Games, providing a widespread network of sports facilities and infrastructures. In the Serra de Collserola, on the slopes of the Tibidabo Hill, the English architect, Lord Norman Foster designed the transmission tower as the coordinating core for all the communication infrastructures in the entire metropolitan area. Built in only two years, the Tower is over 288 metres high, and is the tallest structure in Catalonia. The extremely hi-tech solutions involved the collaboration of local engineers and the international firm, Arup. The main mast is composed of a hollow concrete and reinforced steel cylinder with a diameter of only 4.5 metres. The thirteen floors are surrounded by a continuous stainless steel grid around the perimeter. On the tenth floor is El Mirador, a wonderful viewing platform open to the public with a panorama of the whole city.

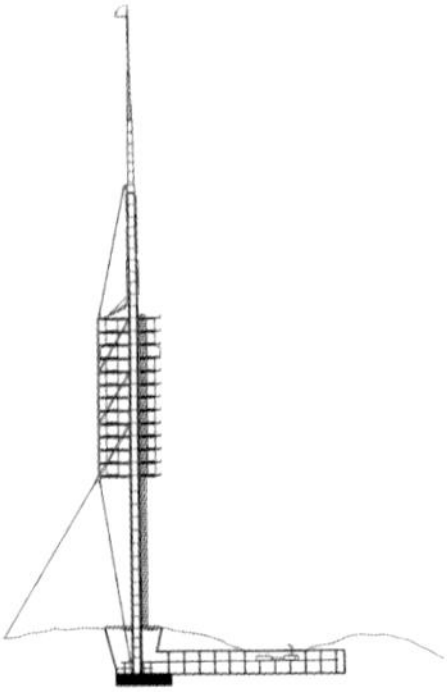

architects
Foster + Partners

type
infrastructure

construction
1992

83. Oak House School

Carrer de Sant Pere Claver, 12-18
08017, Barcelona

open to the public

+34 93 252 40 20
ec@oakhouseschool.com
www.oakhouseschool.com

ES / S1 / S2 >
Peu del Funicular

In 2015, Trasbordo (Justo Orgaz & Ignacio Capapé) designed a school building for the prestigious Oak House School on the steep rocky terrain at the foot of Collserola. The geography of the site and natural landscape were the main inspirations for the project, and from a performance viewpoint, 80% of the building's electrical consumption is provided by geothermal energy. To adapt to the site, the building is composed of rectangular structures set on two different land levels. The diversified structural systems can be clearly seen in the choice of construction materials. The partially buried sections have bearing walls in concrete with very high insulation capacity, and a large part of the roofing is planted and forms pedestrian areas. Separated from the lower floor by a glazed strip, the upper buildings are finished with external insulation and special wood cladding.

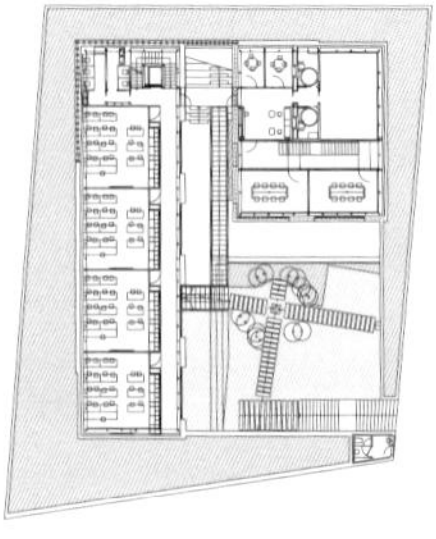

© Trasbordo

© Enrique Cabeza de Vaca

architects
Trasbordo

type
school

construction
2015

84. Lycée Français Maternelle

Carrer de Munner, 5
08022, Barcelona

external viewing only

L7 > Avinguda Tibidabo

The former school complex was composed of several temporary buildings constructed over the years around two early 20th century villas. Because of new practical necessities, it was decided to keep only one of the villas, and to build a new efficient, functional school building.
The last century villa and the new building are separated by a large central courtyard area composed of a play area and green garden space. The two buildings are connected by a covered portico. The new building is spread over 4 floors. A basement floor takes advantage of the change in levels between the courtyard and the street, and the three upper floors house the classrooms, each floor assigned to a different scholastic level. The villa was restored and now houses the common areas, media library, music room and offices. The new building features rounded corners that echo the architectural design of the villa, and the façades are clad in vertical brise soleil slats of different heights, thickness, orientation and colour.

© b720 Fermín Vázquez Arquitectos

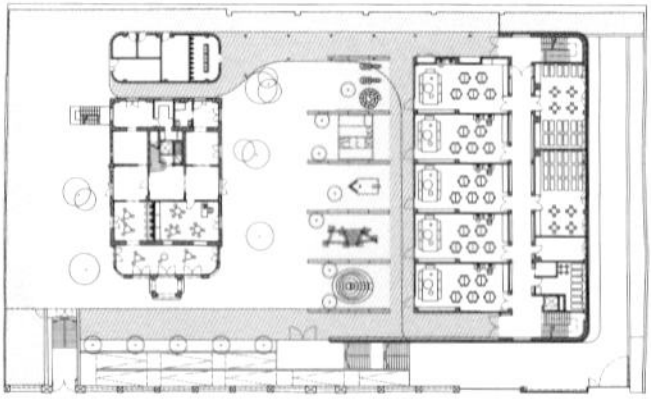

architects
b720 Fermín Vázquez Arquitectos

type
school

construction
2017

85. Biblioteca Sant Gervasi – Joan Maragall

Carrer de Sant Gervasi de Cassoles, 85
08022, Barcelona

Mon, Wed, Fri / 10 am - 2 pm, 4 pm - 8.30 pm
Tue, Thu / 10 am - 8.30 pm
Sat / 10 am - 2 pm
Sun / closed

+34 93 417 83 47

L3 > Vallcarca

The Jardins de Villa Florida occupy a whole urban block in the Sarrià-Sant Gervasi neighbourhood and are composed of three sections: a therapeutic garden, the Joan Maragall district library, and a civic centre located in the early 20th century Villa Florida in Noucentista style. The library was designed by BCQ arquitectura in 2008 following a competition launched in 2007. The library was completed recently and is composed of a series of different structures and patios; the designers used the difference in ground levels in via Sant Gervasi de Cassoles to create an independent entrance. The library buildings are set partially underground and are clad in clay brick to blend with the colour of the surrounding paving. The gardens planted on the library roofs are on the same level as the existing villa gardens.

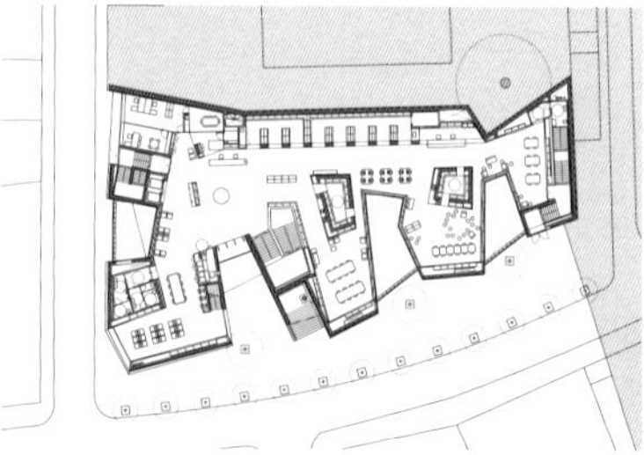

© BCQ arquitectura barcelona

© Ariel Ramírez

architects
BCQ arquitectura barcelona

type
library

construction
2011 - 2014

86. Col·legi Major Sant Jordi

Passatge de
Ricard Zamora, 4
08017, Barcelona

open to the public

+34 93 201 66 00
cmsjordi@cmsantjordi.com
cmsantjordi.ub.edu

L3 > Maria Cristina

The new Sant Jordi university student residence was designed in 2005 by the renowned architect, Josep Lluís Mateo, and is part of a new residential development project. The site was previously a football pitch, and the building is composed of two buildings separated by an internal garden. The tower building houses a student residence and features metal panel cladding with regular rows of window openings. The lower building includes a smaller number of student rooms, an assembly hall, a study area, an indoor basketball court and several common areas for socialising. The façade is a light translucent curtain wall with special light and colour effects designed by the artist Sílvia Hornig.

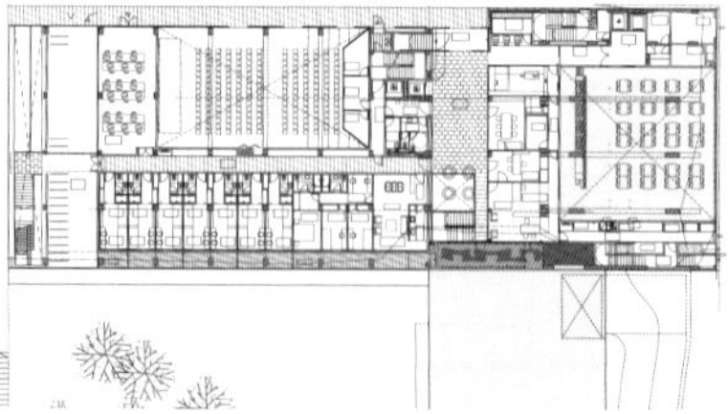

architects
Mateo Arquitectura

type
residential, library, sports centre

construction
2006

Museums

Born Centre de Cultura i Memòria
Cultural and Memorial Centre
of Barcelona
-
Plaça Comercial 12, 08003 Barcelona

elbornculturaimemoria.barcelona.cat
Tel +34 93 256 68 51

CCCB Centre de Cultura Contemporània de Barcelona
Research and Temporary
Exhibition Centre
-
Montalegre 5, 08001 Barcelona

www.cccb.org
info@cccb.org
Tel +34 93 306 41 00

CosmoCaixa
Science Museum
-
Carrer d'Isaac Newton 26,
08022 Barcelona

www.cosmocaixa.es
Tel +34 93 212 60 50

Fundació Antoni Tàpies
Museum of modern and contemporary art
-
Carrer d'Aragó 255, 08007 Barcelona

www.fundaciotapies.org
Tel +34 93 487 03 15

Fundació Joan Miró
Collection of works by the artist Joan Miró
-
Parc de Montjuïc, 08038 Barcelona

www.fmirobcn.org
info@fmirobcn.org
Tel +34 93 443 94 70

Fundació Suñol
Museum of contemporary art
-
Passeig de Gràcia, 98,
08008 Barcelona

www.fundaciosunol.org
info@fundaciosunol.org
Tel +34 93 496 10 32

Jardí Botànic
Botanical Gardens
-
Parc de Montjuïc, Dr. Font i Quer 2,
08038 Barcelona

www.museuciencies.cat
Tel +34 93 256 41 60

MACBA Museu d'Art Contemporani de Barcelona
Museum of modern and contemporary art
-
Plaça dels Àngels 1, 08001 Barcelona

www.macba.cat
Tel +34 93 481 33 68

Museu de Ciències Naturals de Barcelona
Museum of Natural Science
-
Plaça Leonardo da Vinci 4-5,
08019 Barcelona

www.museuciencies.cat
museuciencies@bcn.cat
Tel +34 93 256 60 02

Museu del Disseny de Barcelona
Museum of Design
-
Plaça de les Glòries Catalanes 37,
08018 Barcelona

ajuntament.barcelona.cat/
museudeldisseny
museudeldisseny@bcn.cat
Tel +34 93 256 68 00

Museu del Temple Expiatori de La Sagrada Familia
Historic museum
-
Carrer de Mallorca 401, 08013 Barcelona

www.sagradafamilia.org
informacio@sagradafamilia.org
Tel +34 93 208 04 14

Museu Nacional d'Art de Catalunya
Museum of modern art
-
Palau Nacional, Parc de Montjuïc, s/n,
08038 Barcelona

www.museunacional.cat
Tel +34 93 622 03 60

Pavelló alemany Mies van der Rohe
Contemporary architecture
-
Avinguda Francesc Ferrer i Guàrdia 7,
08038 Barcelona

www.miesbcn.com
pavellomies@miesbcn.com
Tel +34 93 215 10 11

Theatres

Gran Teatre del Liceu

La Rambla 51-59, 08002 Barcelona

www.liceuBarcellona.cat
Tel +34 93 485 99 00

El Molino

Carrer Vilà i Vilà 99,
08004 Barcelona

es.teatrebarcelona.com/el-molino

Mercat de Les Flors

Carrer de Lleida 59, 08004 Barcelona

www.mercatflors.cat/
info@mercatflors.cat
Tel +34 93 256 26 00

Palau de la música

C/ Palau de la Música 4-6,
08003 Barcelona

www.palaumusica.cat/ca
Tel +34 93 295 72 00

Sala Beckett

Carrer de Pere IV 228-232,
08005 Barcelona

www.salabeckett.cat
Tel +34 93 284 53 12

Teatre Goya
-
Carrer de Joaquín Costa 68,
08001 Barcelona

www.teatregoya.cat
info@teatregoya.cat
Tel +34 93 343 53 23

Teatre Lliure
-
Plaça de Margarida Xirgu 1,
08004 Barcelona

www.teatrelliure.com
info@teatrelliure.com
Tel +34 93 238 76 25

Teatre Nacional de Catalunya – TNC
-
Plaça de les Arts 1, 08013 Barcelona

www.tnc.cat
info@tnc.cat
Tel +34 93 306 57 00

Teatre Poliorama
-
Rambla dels Estudis 115,
08002 Barcelona

www.teatrepoliorama.com
suport@teatrepoliorama.com
Tel +34 93 317 75 99

Teatre Romea
-
Carrer de l'Hospital 51, 08001 Barcelona

www.teatreromea.cat
info@teatreromea.com
Tel +34 93 301 55 04

Teatre Tívoli
-
Carrer de Casp 8, 08010 Barcelona

es.teatrebarcelona.com/teatre-tivoli
Tel +34 93 215 95 70

Restaurants

• • • expensive
• • mid-range
• inexpensive

7 portes
• • •
Passeig d'Isabel II 14, 08003 Barcelona

www.7portes.com
reserves@7portes.com
Tel +34 93 319 30 33

Alkimia
• • •
Ronda Sant Antoni 41, 08011 Barcelona

www.alchimiabcn.com
reserves@alkimia.cat
Tel +34 93 207 61 15

Dos Palillos
• • •
Carrer d'Elisabets 9, 08001 Barcelona

www.dospalillos.com
dospalillos@dospalillos.com
Tel +34 93 304 05 13

Tragaluz
• • •
Pasaje de la Concepción 5,
08008 Barcelona

www.grupotragaluz.com
tragaluz@grupotragaluz.com

Cera 23
• •
Carrer de la Cera 23, 08001 Barcelona

www.cera23.com
reservas@cera23.com
Tel +34 93 442 08 08

Cova Fumada
• •
Carrer del Baluart 56, 08003 Barcelona
Tel +34 93 221 40 61

Fàbrica Moritz Barcellona
• •
Ronda Sant Antoni 41, 08011 Barcelona
www.moritz.com
Tel +34 93 426 00 50

Tikets
• •
Avinguda del Paral·lel 164, 08015 Barcelona
info@ticketsbar.es
Tel +34 93 292 42 52

Vinitus
•
Carrer de Consell de Cent 333, 08007 Barcelona
www.vinitusbarcelona.net
admin@vinitusbarcelona.net
Tel +34 93 363 21 27

Wide selection of tapas bars

Carrer Parlament, 08015 Barcelona

Wide selection of restaurants and street food at Mercat Santa Caterina

Avinguda de Francesc Cambó 16, 08003 Barcelona
Tel +34 93 319 57 40

Hotels

• • • expensive
• • mid-range
• inexpensive

Barceló Raval
• •
Rambla del Raval 17-21, 08001 Barcelona
www.barcelo.com
Tel +34 93 320 14 90

Hotel 1898
• •
La Rambla 109, 08001 Barcelona
www.hotel1898.com
1898@nnhotels.com
Tel +34 93 552 95 52

Hotel Porta Fira
• •
Plaça d'Europa 45, 08908 Barcelona
www.hotelbarcelonaportafira.com
reservas.portafira@h-santos.es
Tel +34 93 297 35 00

Mandarin Oriental Barcelona
• •
Passeig de Gràcia 38-40, 08007 Barcelona
www.mandarinoriental.com
mobcn-reservations@mohg.com
Tel +34 93 151 88 88

Meliá Barcelona Sky
•
Carrer de Pere IV 272, 08005 Barcelona
www.melia.com
melia.sky@melia.com
Tel +34 93 367 20 50

W Barcelona
• • •
Plaça de la Rosa dels Vents, 1 Final, Passeig de Joan de Borbó, 08039 Barcelona
Tel +34 93 295 28 00

Ako Suite Hotel
• •
Carrer de la Diputació 195, 08011 Barcelona
www.akosuite.com
info@akosuite.com
Tel +34 93 453 34 19

Axel Hotel
• •
Carrer d'Aribau 33, 08011 Barcelona
www.axelhotels.com
barcelona@axelhotels.com
Tel +34 93 323 93 93

Hotel SERHS Carlit
• •
Carrer de la Diputació 383, 08013 Barcelona
www.hotelserhscarlit.com
info.carlit@grupserhs.com
Tel +34 93 505 26 00

Hotel Constanza
•
Carrer del Bruc 33, 08010 Barcelona
www.hotelconstanza.com
info@hotelconstanza.com
Tel +34 93 270 19 10

Hotel Curious
•
Carrer del Carme 25, 08001 Barcelona
www.hotelcurious.com
hotel@hotelcurious.com
Tel +34 93 301 44 84

Hotel Oasis
•
Pla de Palau 17, 08003 Barcelona
www.hoteloasisbarcelona.com
reservas@hoteloasis.es
Tel +34 93 319 43 96

Architectural offices

AIA Salazar Navarro
Plaça Sant Pere 3, 08003 Barcelona
www.aia.cat
Tel +34 93 412 05 14

Albert Viaplana Veà
Aribau 318 atico 1, 08006 Barcelona
www.viaplana.com
Tel +34 93 200 61 75

aldayjover arquitectura y paisaje
Avinguda Portal de l'Àngel 3-5, 08002 Barcelona
www.aldayjover.com
Tel +34 934 121 663

Alonso y Balaguer
Carrer Pellaires 30-38, 08019 Barcelona
www.alonsobalaguer.com
Tel +34 93 303 41 60

b720 Fermín Vázquez Arquitectos
Calvet 55, E-08021 Barcelona
www.b720.com
Tel +34 93 363 79 79

BAAS Arquitectura
Montserrat de Casanovas 105,
08032 Barcelona
www.baas.cat
Tel +34 93 358 01 11

BCQ arquitectura barcelona
Carrer Vallirana 30,
08006 Barcelona
www.bcq.es
Tel +34 93 237 27 21

Brullet-de Luna i Associats
Avinguda Coll del Portell 52,
08024 Barcelona
www.brulletdeluna.com
Tel +34 93 210 53 01

Calderon-Folch Studio
Espaseria 15, 08003 Barcelona
www.cfs.cat
Tel +34 93 141 49 37

CMV Architects
Via Augusta 13-15 pl 7ª oficina 702,
08006 Barcelona
www.cmv-architects.com
Tel +34 97 172 08 39

EMBA – Estudi Massip-Bosch Architects
Balmes 307, 08006 Barcelona
www.emba.cat
Tel +34 93 211 22 68

Enric Ruiz Geli / Cloud 9 studio
Carrer dels Caponata 8,
08034 Barcelona
www.ruiz-geli.com

Estudio Carme Pinós
Avinguda Diagonal 490,
08006 Barcelona
www.cpinos.com
Tel +34 93 416 03 72

Flores Prats Architects
Carrer de Trafalgar 12, 08010 Barcelona
www.floresprats.com
Tel +34 93 2684635

Forgas Arquitectes
Diputació 337, 08009 Barcelona
www.forgasarquitectes.com
Tel +34 93 232 56 31

Garcés - De Seta - Bonet, Arquitectes
Carrer d'en Quintana 4,
08002 Barcelona
www.garces-deseta-bonet.com
Tel +34 93 317 31 88

Ansana, de la Villa, de Paauw, Arquitectes
Avinguda Portal de l'Àngel 7,
08002 Barcelona
www.jdvdp.com
Tel +34 93 317 21 07

Jorge Vidal
Bonistrol 25, 08012 Barcelona
www.jorgevidal.eu
Tel +34 93 017 46 43

Luís Cantallops
Passeig de Sant Joan 42,
08010 Barcelona
www.cantallopsvicente.com
Tel +34 93 412 43 00

MAIO
Bruniquer 23, 08012 Barcelona
www.maio-architects.com
Tel +34 93 213 87 70

Manuel Rui Sánchez
Avinguda Diagonal 622,
08021 Barcelona
www.ruisanchez.net
Tel +34 93 414 16 14

Martínez Lapeña-Torres Arquitectos
Roca i Batlle 14, 08023 Barcelona
Tel +34 93 212 14 16

Mateo Arquitectura
Teodor Roviralta 39,
08022 Barcelona
www.mateo-arquitectura.com
Tel +34 93 218 63 58

MBM ARQUITECTES
Plaça Reial 18,
08002 Barcelona
www.mbmarquitectes.cat
Tel +34 93 317 00 61

MIAS Arquitectes
www.miasarquitectes.com
Tel +34 93 238 82 08

Miralles Tagliabue EMBT
Passatge de la Pau 10,
08002 Barcelona
www.mirallestagliabue.com
Tel +34 93 412 53 42

Nomen arquitectes i associats
C/ Provença 249, 08008 Barcelona
Tel +34 93 415 78 60

OAB – Office of Architecture in Barcelona
Carrer Balmes 145,
08008 Barcelona
www.ferrater.com
Tel +34 93 238 51 36

Pau Vidal
Pere IV 29-35-5-1,
08018 Barcelona
www.pauvidal.eu
Tel +34 67 901 74 46

Picharchitects
Àvila 138, 08018 Barcelona
www.picharchitects.com
Tel +34 93 301 64 57

PINEARQ – Albert de Pineda
C/ Mare de Déu de la Salut 40,
08024 Barcelona
www.pinearq.es
Tel +34 93 210 68 19

Ravetllat Ribas
Rambla de Catalunya 11,
08007 Barcelona
www.ravetllatribas.com
Tel +34 93 280 26 90

Ricard Galiana Nadal
C/ Francisco Giner 22,
08012 Barcelona
www.ricardgaliana.com
Tel +34 93 515 42 47

Roldán+Berengué, Arquitectes
Girona 37, 08010 Barcelona
www.roldanberengue.com
Tel +34 93 301 06 96

RQP arquitectura
Passeig de la Bonanova 9,
08022 Barcelona
www.rqparquitectura.com
Tel +34 93 43 43 20

Ruisánchez Arquitectes
Avinguda Diagonal 622,
08021 Barcelona
www.ruisanchez.net
Tel +34 93 414 16 14

Saeta Estudi
Passeig Sant Joan 12,
08010 Barcelona
www.saetaestudi.com
Tel +34 93 247 65 62

Sergi Godia
Carrer Doctor Fleming 4,
08017 Barcelona
www.sergigodia.net
Tel +34 69 628 27 01

ergi Pons architects
Avinguda Diagonal 401,
08008 Barcelona
www.sergiponsarchitect.com
Tel +34 93 185 17 69

UMO Arquitectes
arrer Ausiàs Marc 26,
8010 Barcelona
www.sumo-arquitectes.com
Tel +34 93 318 13 73

erradas Arquitectos
Paseo Manuel Girona 75,
8034 Barcelona
www.terradasarquitectos.com
Tel +34 93 204 80 66

erritori24
/Església 4-10,
8024 Barcelona
www.territori24.com
Tel +34 93 238 87 18

íctor Rahola
arrer de Girona, 8,
8010 Barcelona
www.victorrahola.cat
Tel +34 93 244 85 50

ora
ant Pere Més alt 62,
8003 Barcelona
www.vora.cat
Tel +34 93 553 39 19

Index by architect

Index by project

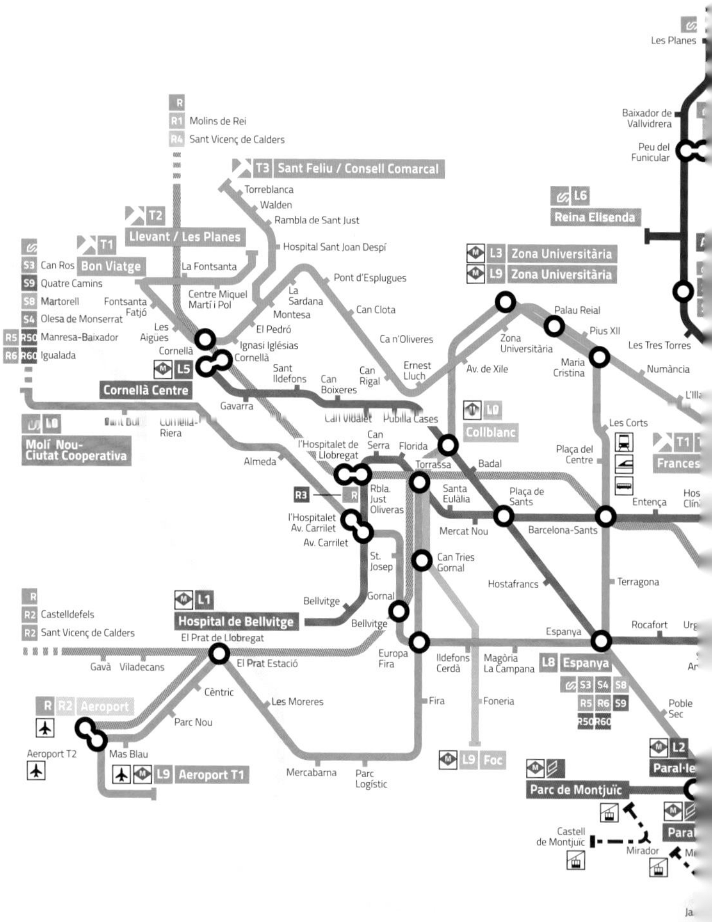
Les Planes
Baixador de Vallvidrera
Peu del Funicular
R
R1 Molins de Rei
R4 Sant Vicenç de Calders
T3 Sant Feliu / Consell Comarcal
Torreblanca
Walden
Rambla de Sant Just
Hospital Sant Joan Despí
L6 Reina Elisenda
T2 Llevant / Les Planes
T1 Bon Viatge
S3 Can Ros
S9 Quatre Camins
S8 Martorell
S4 Olesa de Monserrat
R5 R50 Manresa-Baixador
R6 R60 Igualada
La Fontsanta
Fontsanta Fatjó
Centre Miquel Martí i Pol
La Sardana
Montesa
El Pedró
Pont d'Esplugues
Can Clota
Ca n'Oliveres
L3 Zona Universitària
L9 Zona Universitària
Palau Reial
Pius XII
Les Tres Torres
Numància
Zona Universitària
Maria Cristina
Av. de Xile
Ernest Lluch
Can Rigal
Can Boixeres
Sant Ildefons
Ignasi Iglésias
Cornellà
Les Aigües
Cornellà
L5 Cornellà Centre
Gavarra
Can Vidalet
Pubilla Cases
L8 Molí Nou-Ciutat Cooperativa
Sant Boi
Cornellà-Riera
Almeda
L9 Collblanc
Les Corts
Plaça del Centre
T1 Frances
L'Illa
Can Serra
Florida
l'Hospitalet de Llobregat
Torrassa
Badal
R3
R
Rbla. Just Oliveras
Santa Eulàlia
Plaça de Sants
Entença
Hos Clín
l'Hospitalet Av. Carrilet
Av. Carrilet
Mercat Nou
Barcelona-Sants
St. Josep
Can Tries Gornal
Hostafrancs
Terragona
Gornal
Bellvitge
Bellvitge
L1 Hospital de Bellvitge
R
R2 Castelldefels
R2 Sant Vicenç de Calders
El Prat de Llobregat
El Prat Estació
Gavà
Viladecans
Europa Fira
Ildefons Cerdà
Magòria La Campana
Espanya
L8 Espanya
S3 S4 S8
R5 R6 S9
R50 R60
Rocafort
Urg
Ar
Cèntric
Les Moreres
Fira
Foneria
Poble Sec
R R2 Aeroport
Parc Nou
Aeroport T2
Mas Blau
L9 Aeroport T1
Mercabarna
Parc Logístic
L9 Foc
L2 Paral·le
Parc de Montjuïc
Castell de Montjuïc
Mirador
Paral
Ja

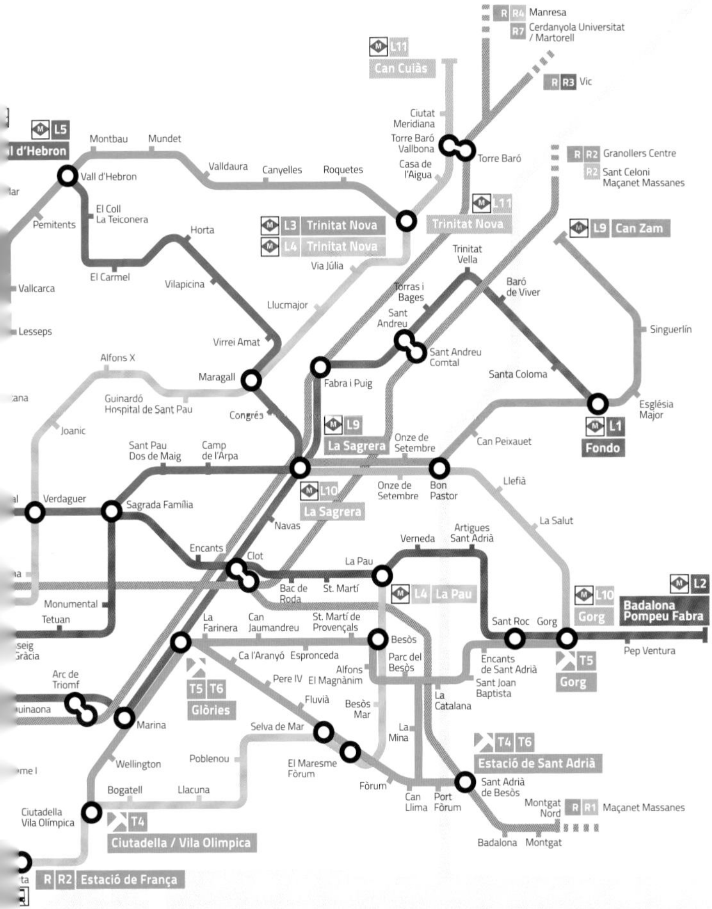

- L1 Hospital de Bellvitge / Fondo
- L2 Paral·lel / Badalona Pompeau Fabra
- L3 Zona Universitària / Trinitat Nova
- L4 La Pau / Trinitat Nova
- L5 Cornellà Centre / Vall d'Hebron
- L9 La Sagrera / Can Zam
- L9 Aeroport T1 / Zona Universitària
- L10 La Sagrera / Gorg
- L10 Foc / Collblanc
- L11 Trinitat Nova / Can Cuiàs
- FM Paral·lel / Parc de Montjuïc

This volume was printed in February 2019
by CPZ Group, Costa di Mezzate (BG), Italy